CALL ME Bill

LYNETTE RICHARDS

EMANATA

Call Me Bill

First Edition

Printed by Gauvin in Quebec, Canada on recycled papers

#1 in the Emanata Imprint from Conundrum Press
Editor: Sal Sawler
Publisher: Andy Brown

EMANATA graphic novels rely on a seamless blend of words and pictures to tell compelling, character-driven fiction and non-fiction stories. By focusing on work created by comic artists living in Canada and striving for social equity, EMANATA seeks to introduce fresh, strong, and under-represented voices to the international young adult and graphic novel markets.

Library and Archives Canada Cataloguing in Publication

Title: Call me Bill / Lynette Richards.
Names: Richards, Lynette, author, artist.
Identifiers: Canadiana 20220147469 | ISBN 9781772620788 (softcover)
Subjects: LCGFT: Graphic novels.
Classification: LCC PN6733.R53 C35 2022 | DDC j741.5/971—dc23

Conundrum Press
Wolfville, NS
www.conundrumpress.com

Conundrum Press is located in Mi'kma'ki, the ancestral and unceded territory of the Mi'kmaq People

Conundrum Press acknowledges the financial support of the Canada Council for the Arts, the Province of Nova Scotia, and the Government of Canada toward its publishing activities

Canada Council for the Arts
Conseil des Arts du Canada
NOVA SCOTIA

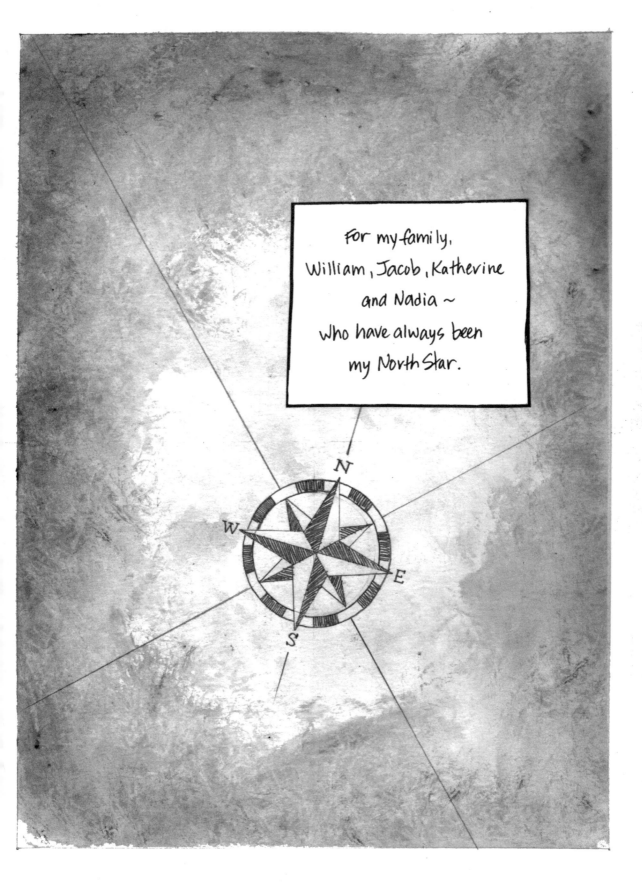

For my family,
William, Jacob, Katherine
and Nadia ~
who have always been
my North Star.

ACKNOWLEDGEMENTS

I am grateful to the following people for your assistance during the four years it took to make this book: Ariella Pahlke; Catherine Phoenix; Daniel MacKay; Emily Burton; John Corbett; Kathy Kaulbach; Lis Van Berkel; Nadia Tymoshenko; Nathaniel Smith; Sal Sawler; and Andy Brown.

Thanks to diver and historian, Bob Chaulk, for your research, books, and tireless efforts to discern facts from folklore, and keep this important event in our memory.

Many of the paintings in this book reference newspaper engravings and rare, precious photographs.

Thanks to the Nova Scotia Archives, and the S.S. Atlantic Heritage Park and Society, for preserving history so we may remember and learn.

Thank you to journalists for your curiosity and your important work of documenting life, including Ralph Keeler (a friend of Mark Twain's), whose interview article forms the skeleton of this story.

My deepest respect is for the villagers, who rose from their beds at 3 a.m. on April 1, 1873 and saved as many lives as they could from an unimaginable disaster. Their courageous and compassionate response to strangers in need of help is an iconic Nova Scotian and Canadian story that should be celebrated forever.

And lastly, I am deeply indebted to the countless people throughout history who defied gender constraints to live authentic lives. I am honoured to bring one such story into the light.

Our protagonist is buried with more than 250 other bodies in the mass grave in Terence Bay, Nova Scotia. The same number are interred in the Catholic cemetery in Lower Prospect, Nova Scotia.

INTRODUCTION

In *Call Me Bill,* Lynette Richards offers a new lens through which to view the tragedy of the sinking of the *SS Atlantic* off the coast of Nova Scotia in 1873. Published 150 years after the shipwreck, and an important part of the anniversary commemorations, the graphic novel helps readers understand the role of the three communities of Terence Bay, Lower Prospect and Upper Prospect in the rescue and recovery efforts. *Call Me Bill* begins and ends with the sinking of the *SS Atlantic*, but focuses on one of the sailors on board the ship who was reported to be a woman named Bill after dying in the shipwreck.

Call Me Bill is a fictionalized account of the life of Maggie/Bill, and the people and places that were part of their world. It is rooted in historical knowledge of the world of the 1860s and 1870s, as well as evidence of the life and identity of "William/Margaret" or "Maggie/Bill" Armstrong from a selection of primary historical sources, including the *Aberdeen Journal* and the *New York Tribune*, as well as a *Halifax Morning Chronicle* article from 1873 about the shipwreck. This last article conveyed to readers the identity of a drowned American sailor who, upon discovery, was found to have breasts, and whom a crew member referred to as "Bill," describing him as "a fellow sailor who used to take his liquor as regular as any of us."

Was this Bill the same Bill described in the other newspapers? The *Aberdeen Journal,* published 22 January, 1873, described a "lady sailor" who arrived in Aberdeen, Scotland, from Malaga, Spain on the ship *Eskdale* of Whitby. Margaret Armstrong, who assumed the name William Armstrong, was from a Dutch New Jersey family, and had decided to become a sailor after her mother died and her father remarried. Nineteen-year old Bill sailed from New York to London in the summer of 1872, and then as an apprentice on board the *Eskdale* with a Mediterranean destination. The captain's wife suspected Bill's other identity, and he had to return to Scotland as Margaret, where she was discharged. The article speculates that the American Consul would "doubtless" provide Margaret with a passage back to New York.

We see a similar historical narrative in a letter to the editor of the *New York Tribune* written by Ralph Keeler from 14 February, 1873. Keeler, himself well-acquainted with a life lived beyond established norms and expectations, took an interest in the young Maggie, alias Billy, Armstrong. Keeler's description also provides biographical details about our young protagonist's life, such as growing up on the farm in New Jersey, how and why Maggie left the farm, Bill's seafaring travels and adventures, and Bill's talk with the captain's wife following an onboard altercation with a "brute of a sailor."

It is likely that Bill, the American sailor who died tragically in the wreck of *SS Atlantic*, was the same person as the sailor described in other historical sources, especially given dates and timing, as well as the similarities in identity. As a work of creative non-fiction, *Call Me Bill* invites readers to imagine this into being. The narrative conveys a truth about the experience of living a non-conformist gender identity in the nineteenth century. Due to this shifting gender identity, we know more about Bill's life, identity, and even inner thoughts, than many other sailors of the time. Keeler, for instance, conveys Maggie's sense of her own "wild, passionate nature," as well as her wish that she were a man.

The experiences documented in historical sources are wonderfully brought to life through the text and illustrations that form the middle sections of the graphic novel, including Keeler's conversations with Maggie on her return voyage to New York. *Call Me Bill* weaves together fact and fiction to create a compelling narrative about an ordinary, extraordinary person who refused to live a life of gender conformity. It does not overreach by attempting to move Maggie/Bill out of the nineteenth century, but brings the known and imagined to life through an accessible narrative. The graphic story allows us to imagine the remarkable resilience required to survive in a sometimes unforgiving world.

Richards' touching tale speaks to the silences in the historical records about lives lived but not acknowledged or remembered. It is an insistence from the author's perspective of recognition across the divides of time that Bill, and others like him, existed, and mattered. *Call Me Bill* is a story that matters. These narratives have always been there, patiently waiting for people like Lynette Richards to understand their importance, and to have the insights and artistry to bring them to life.

Maggie/Bill was a young person willing to take risks to broaden their inner and outer worlds. The novel is embedded in other, more public, nineteenth-century struggles, including winning women's right to vote, and anti-slavery campaigns in the United States. We see slavery through the eyes of both Maggie's Quaker, social reformist mother, and the family's housekeeper, Cicely, who had been formerly enslaved and who advises Maggie to choose her battles. Cicely's husband managed the family's farm, but we do not learn more about Cicely's family or history. There is a discomfort in seeing Cicely through Maggie's eyes. What thoughts did Cicely keep to herself about her life on the farm with Maggie's family, or her aspirations for her own life?

Readers also travel through the Mediterranean and Atlantic worlds of the mid-late nineteenth century, including the seaport alehouses, where we see (again?) that Bill could drink beer like any other alehouse "fellow." We see glimpses of New York, Aberdeen, Liverpool, and London. Through these travels and other life experiences, *Call Me Bill* offers the reader vignettes of sadness and wonder through Maggie and Bill's internal dialogues. We see how Maggie's "body ached" after her brother died, and her bitterness when her father's new wife forced her to stop wearing her brother's clothes. We witness Bill's reflection on the "star-riddled heavens" of eternity after leaving the New Jersey farm to venture into an unknown future, and his sad description of the seals welcoming him home in the cold waters off Marrs Island during the sinking of the *SS Atlantic*.

Richards, a stained glass artist as well as a graphic novelist, who identifies as a feminist lesbian, has the tools in her toolbox to bring this story to light with mastery and empathy. *Call Me Bill* asks us to imagine what it would have been like to be a woman living as a man in the early 1870s. It points to the stories that seemed lost to the historical record, but were actually waiting to be uncovered. Stories that require the proper eyes to see. History is always in the past, but our understandings of the past are always rooted in the present.

— *Emily Burton Rocha, PhD*

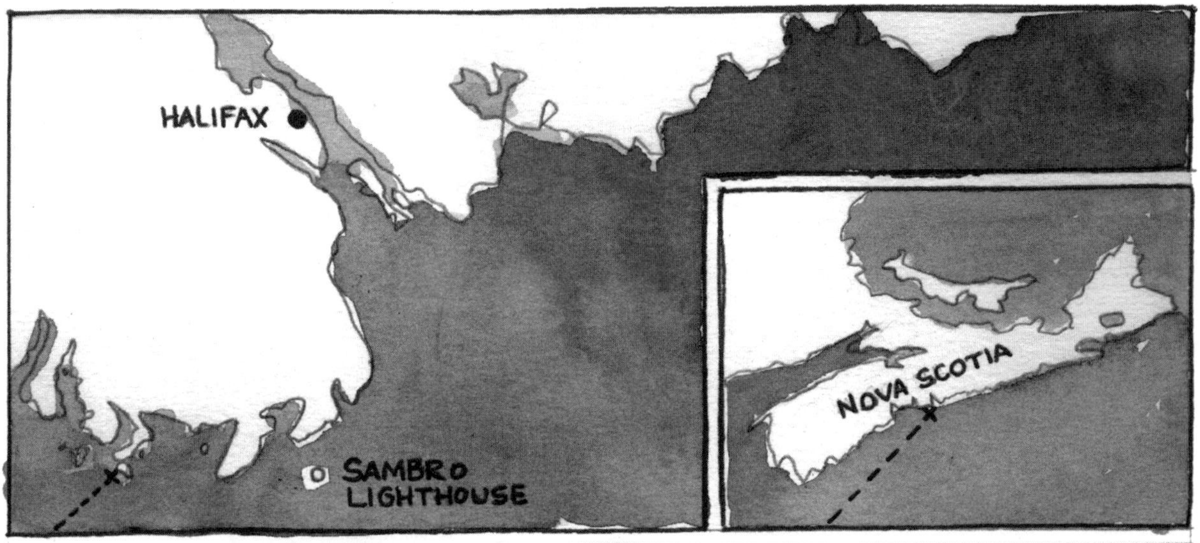
HALIFAX
SAMBRO LIGHTHOUSE
NOVA SCOTIA

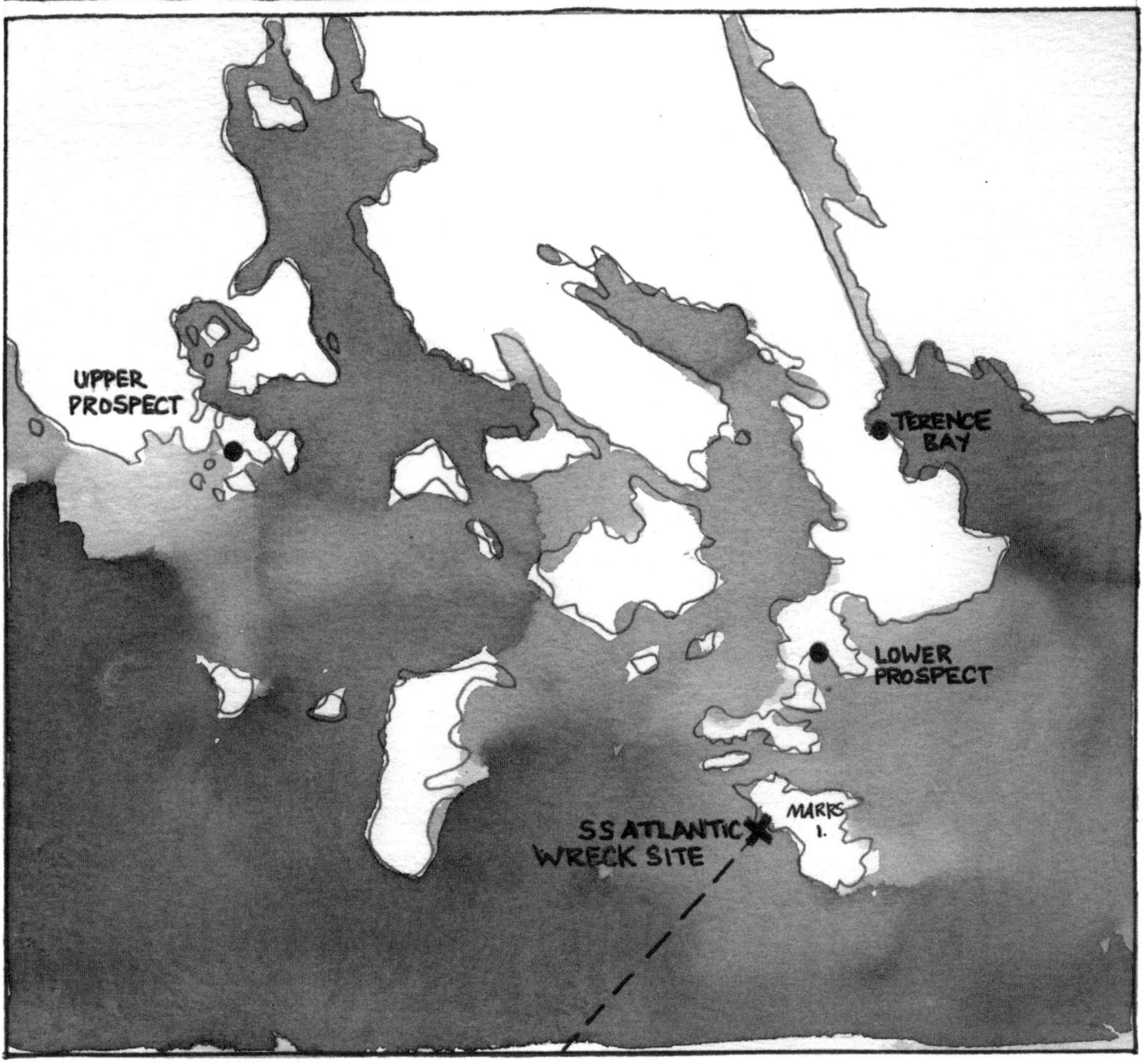
UPPER PROSPECT
TERENCE BAY
LOWER PROSPECT
MARRS I.
SS ATLANTIC WRECK SITE

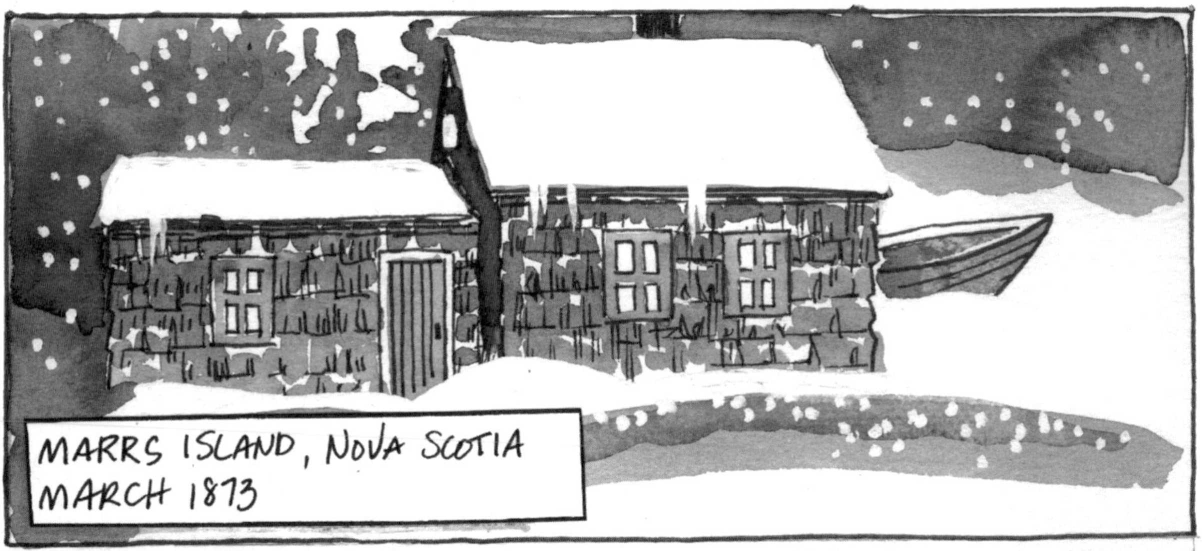
MARRS ISLAND, NOVA SCOTIA
MARCH 1873

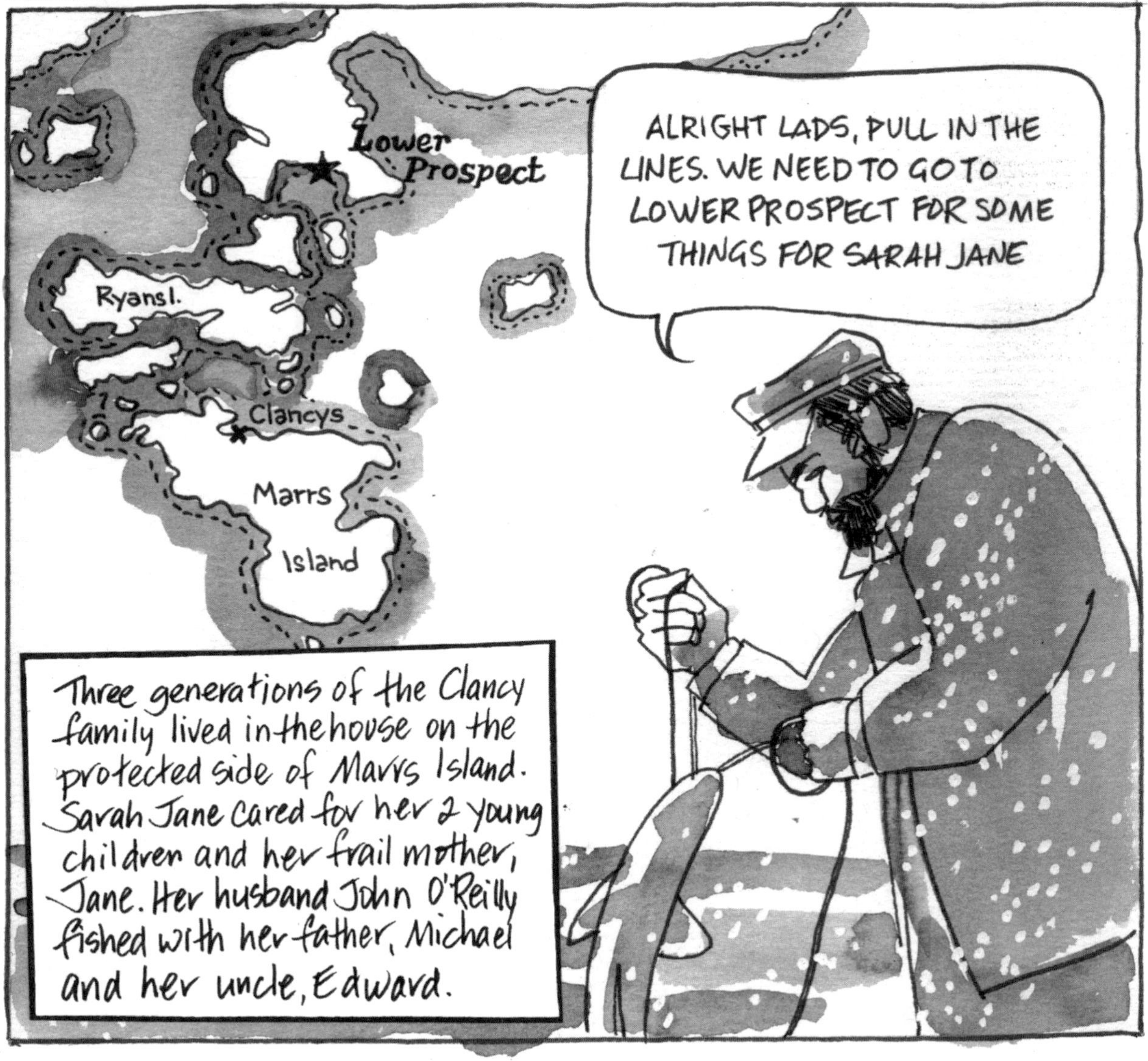
Lower Prospect
Ryans I.
Clancys
Marrs Island
ALRIGHT LADS, PULL IN THE LINES. WE NEED TO GO TO LOWER PROSPECT FOR SOME THINGS FOR SARAH JANE
Three generations of the Clancy family lived in the house on the protected side of Marrs Island. Sarah Jane cared for her 2 young children and her frail mother, Jane. Her husband John O'Reilly fished with her father, Michael and her uncle, Edward.

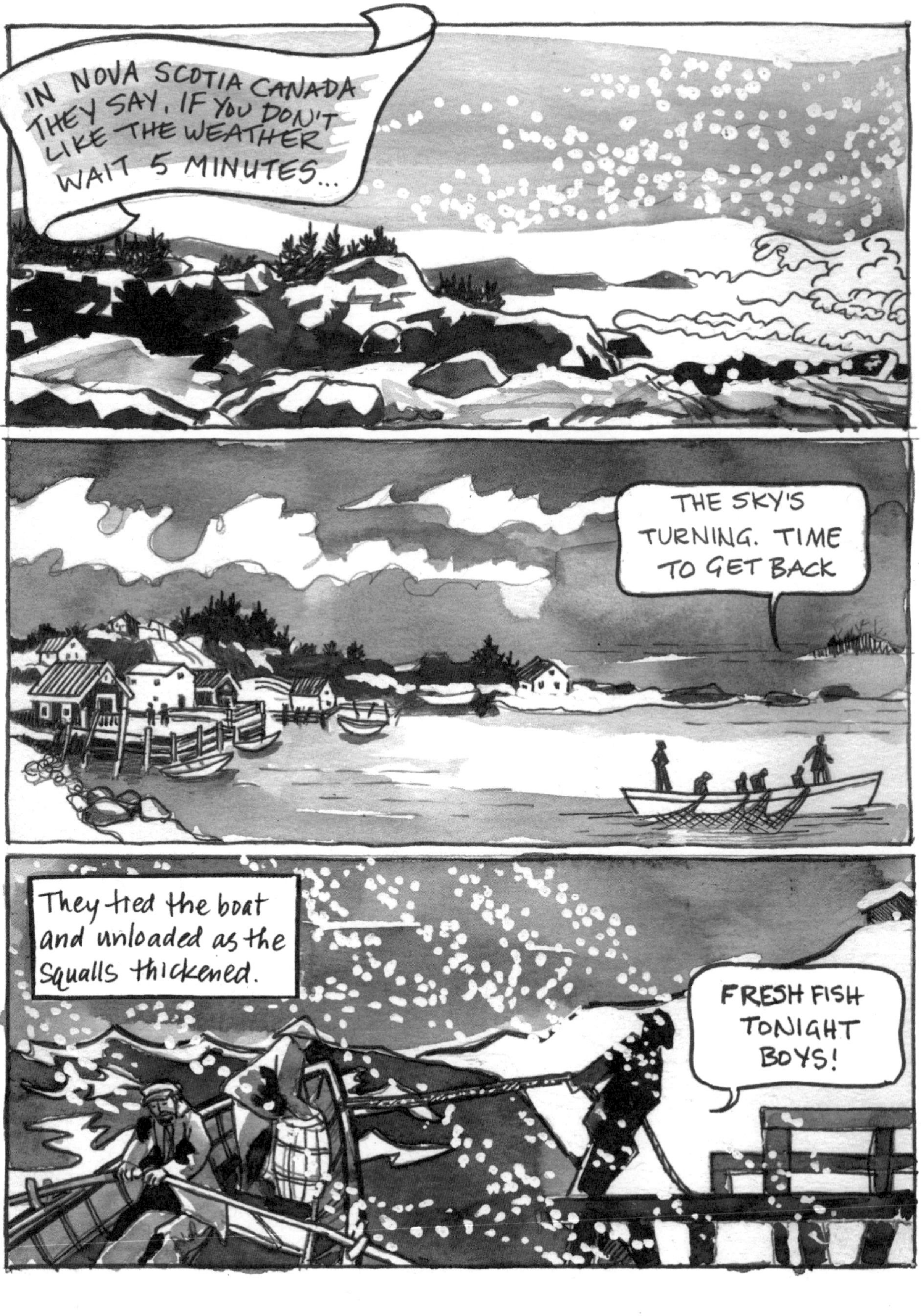
IN NOVA SCOTIA CANADA THEY SAY, IF YOU DON'T LIKE THE WEATHER WAIT 5 MINUTES...
THE SKY'S TURNING. TIME TO GET BACK
They tied the boat and unloaded as the squalls thickened.
FRESH FISH TONIGHT BOYS!

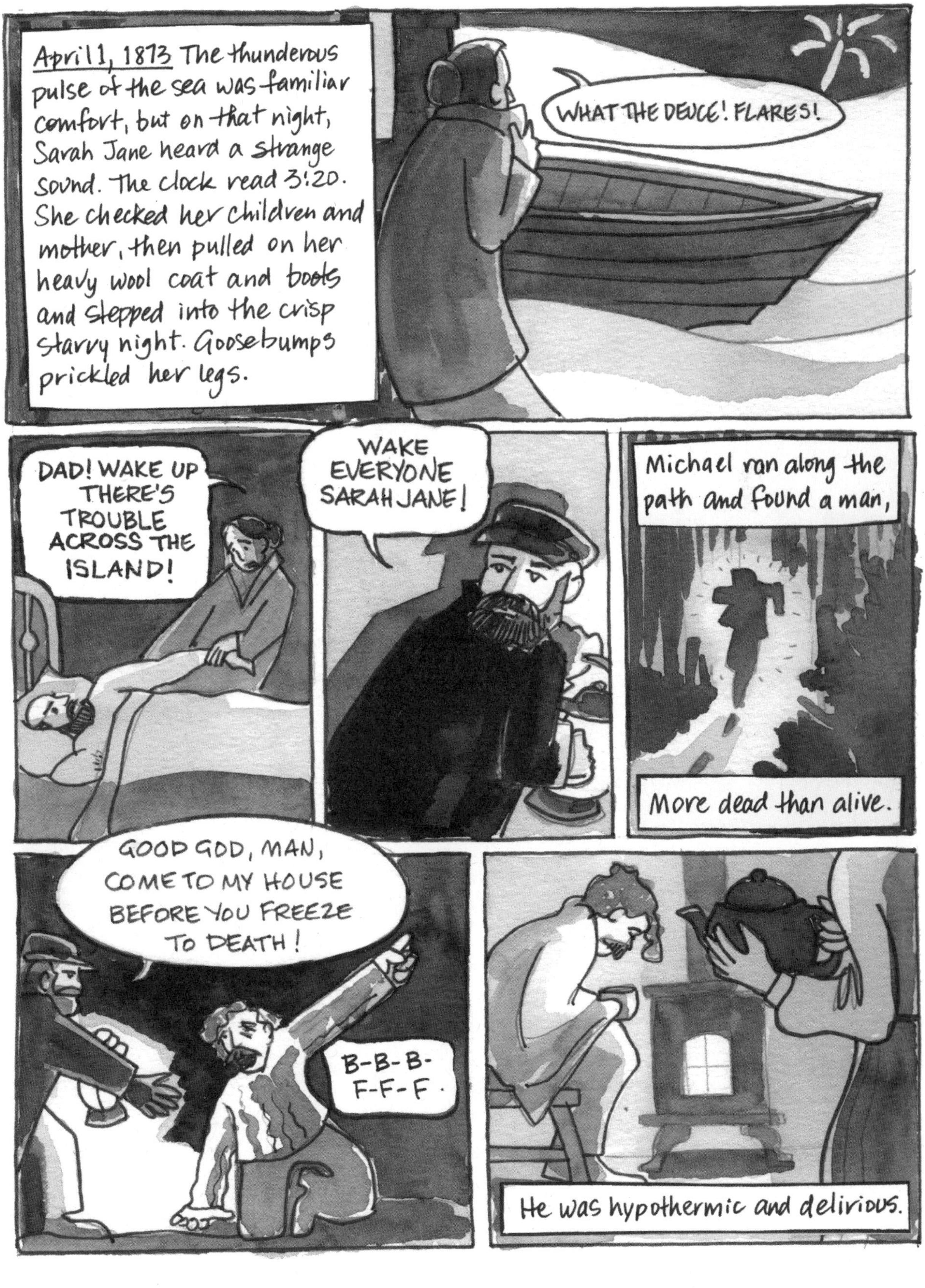
April 1, 1873 The thunderous pulse of the sea was familiar comfort, but on that night, Sarah Jane heard a strange sound. The clock read 3:20. She checked her children and mother, then pulled on her heavy wool coat and boots and stepped into the crisp starry night. Goosebumps prickled her legs.
WHAT THE DEUCE! FLARES!
DAD! WAKE UP THERE'S TROUBLE ACROSS THE ISLAND!
WAKE EVERYONE SARAH JANE!
Michael ran along the path and found a man,
More dead than alive.
GOOD GOD, MAN, COME TO MY HOUSE BEFORE YOU FREEZE TO DEATH!
B-B-B-
F-F-F.
He was hypothermic and delirious.

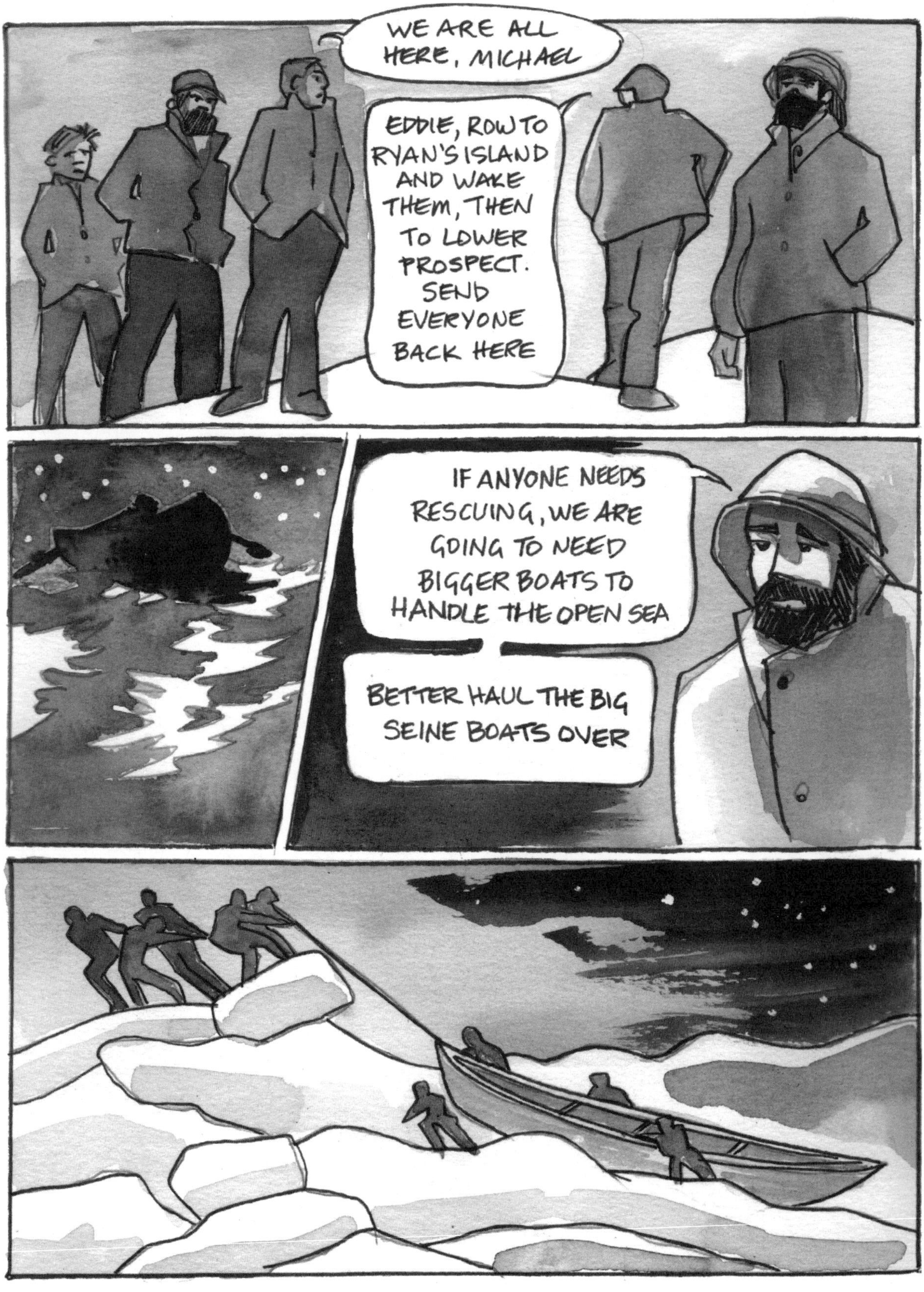
WE ARE ALL HERE, MICHAEL
EDDIE, ROW TO RYAN'S ISLAND AND WAKE THEM, THEN TO LOWER PROSPECT. SEND EVERYONE BACK HERE
IF ANYONE NEEDS RESCUING, WE ARE GOING TO NEED BIGGER BOATS TO HANDLE THE OPEN SEA
BETTER HAUL THE BIG SEINE BOATS OVER

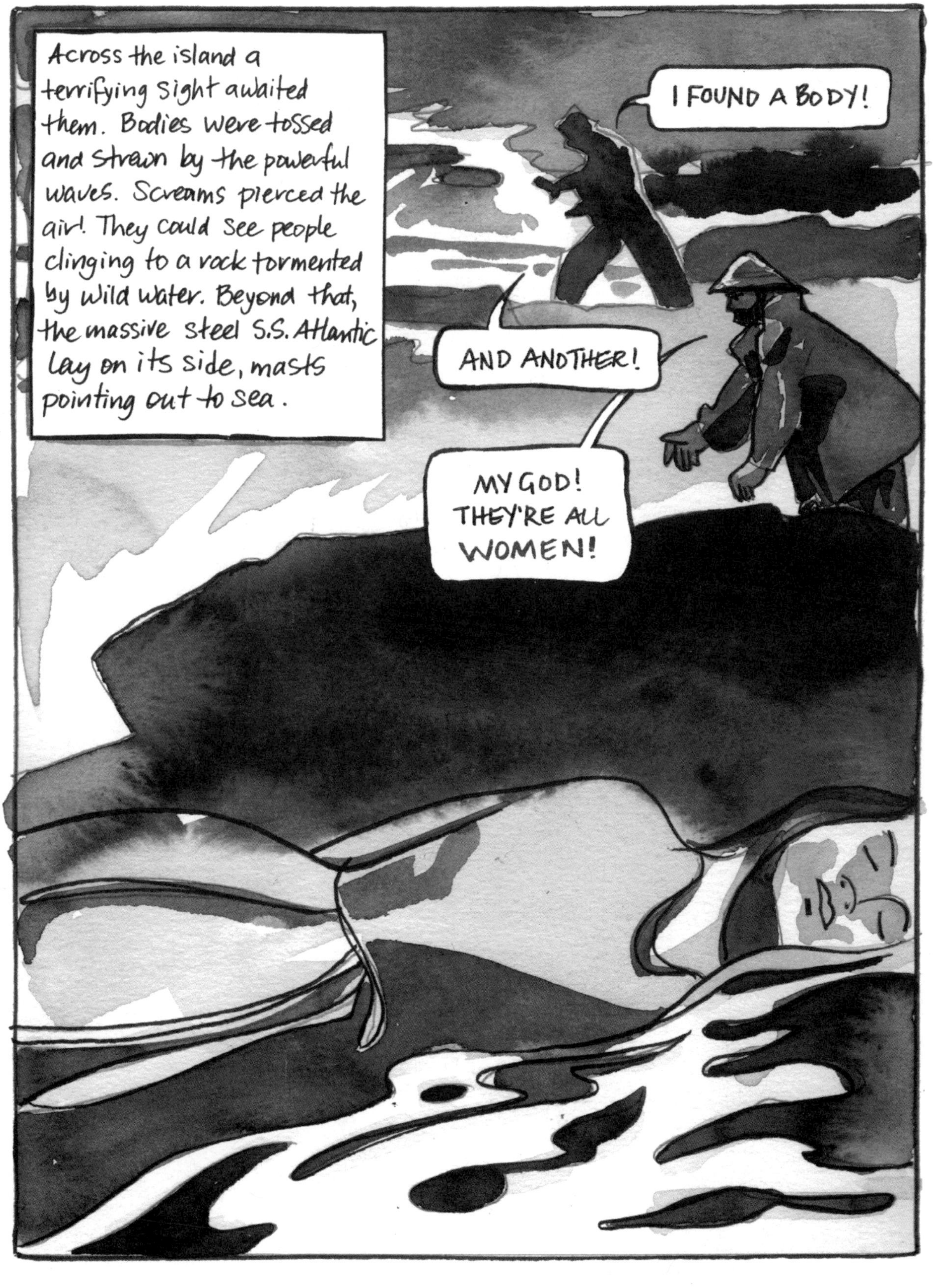
Across the island a terrifying sight awaited them. Bodies were tossed and strewn by the powerful waves. Screams pierced the air! They could see people clinging to a rock tormented by wild water. Beyond that, the massive steel S.S. Atlantic lay on its side, masts pointing out to sea.
I FOUND A BODY!
AND ANOTHER!
MY GOD! THEY'RE ALL WOMEN!

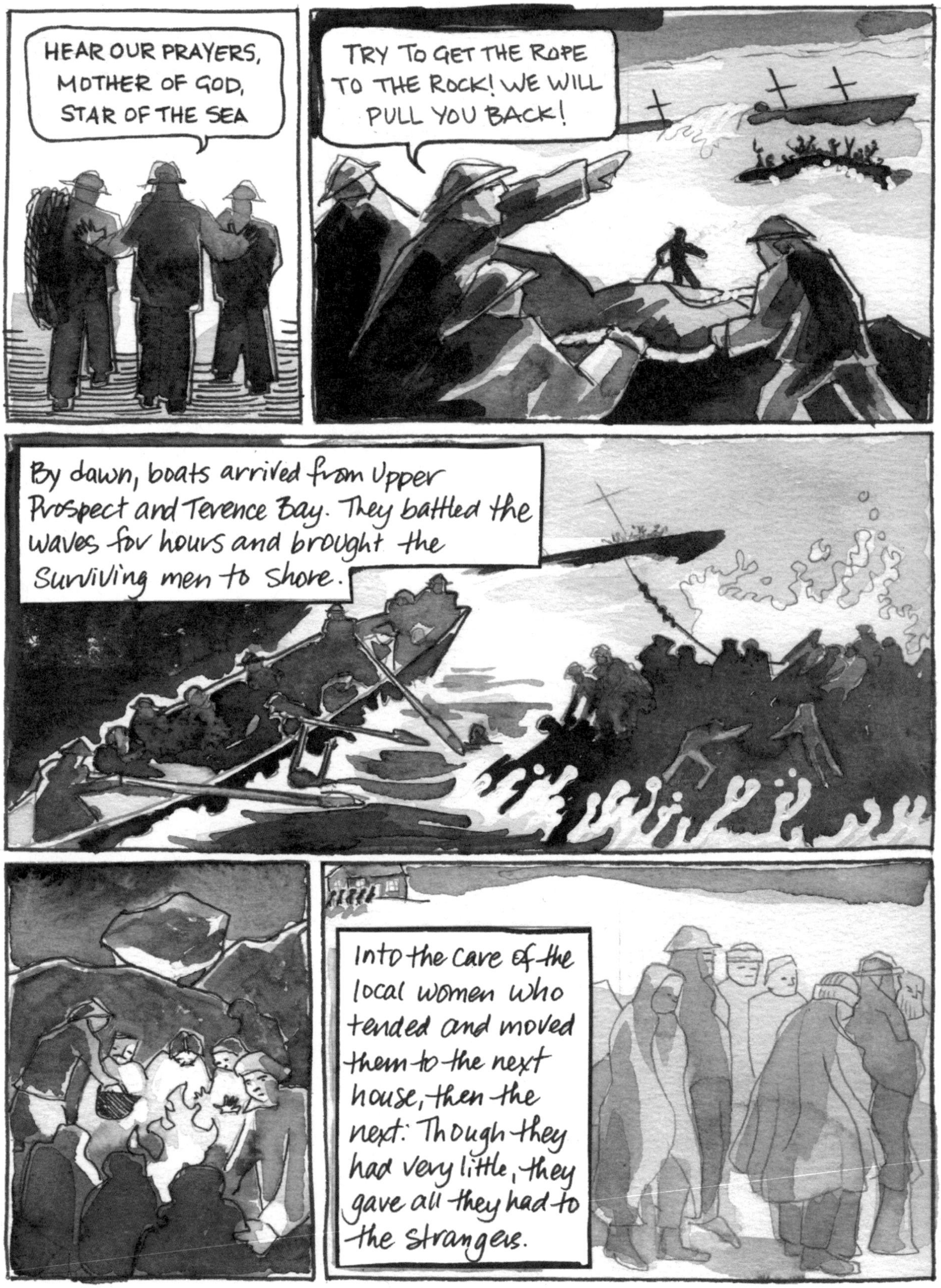
HEAR OUR PRAYERS, MOTHER OF GOD, STAR OF THE SEA
TRY TO GET THE ROPE TO THE ROCK! WE WILL PULL YOU BACK!
By dawn, boats arrived from Upper Prospect and Terence Bay. They battled the waves for hours and brought the surviving men to shore.
Into the care of the local women who tended and moved them to the next house, then the next. Though they had very little, they gave all they had to the strangers.

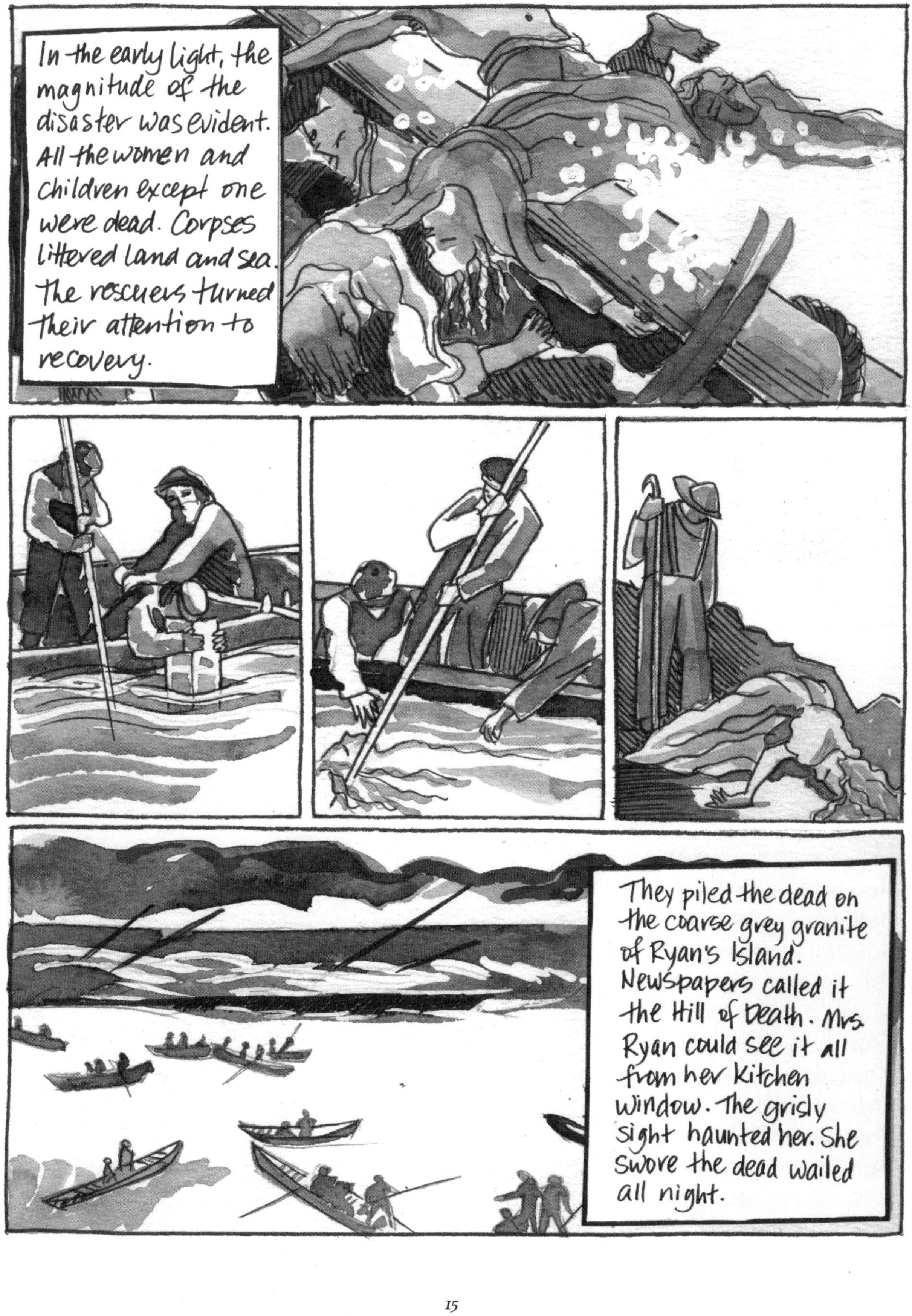
In the early light, the magnitude of the disaster was evident. All the women and children except one were dead. Corpses littered land and sea. The rescuers turned their attention to recovery.
They piled the dead on the coarse grey granite of Ryan's Island. Newspapers called it the Hill of Death. Mrs. Ryan could see it all from her kitchen window. The grisly sight haunted her. She swore the dead wailed all night.

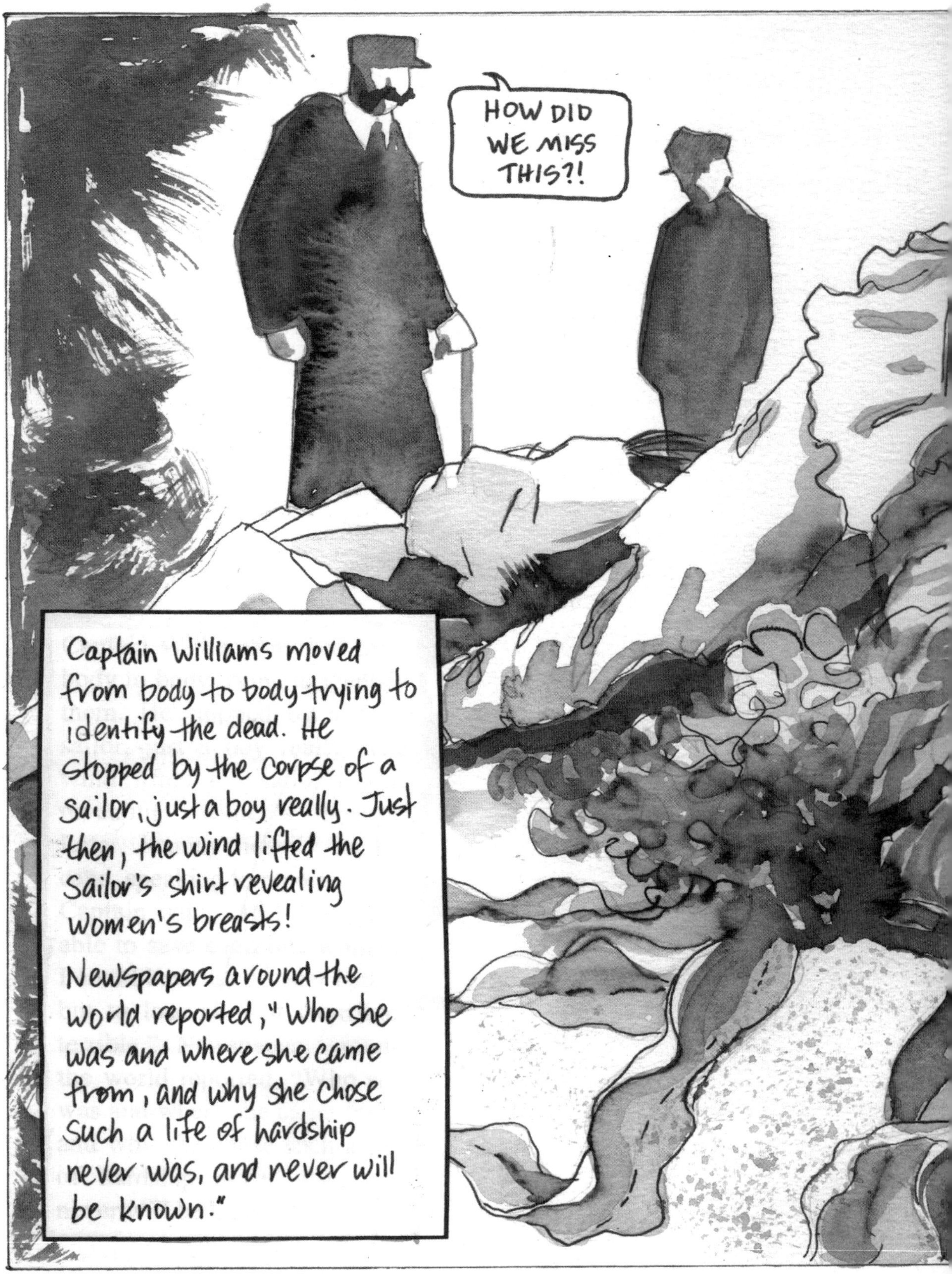
HOW DID WE MISS THIS?!
Captain Williams moved from body to body trying to identify the dead. He stopped by the corpse of a sailor, just a boy really. Just then, the wind lifted the sailor's shirt revealing women's breasts!
Newspapers around the world reported, "Who she was and where she came from, and why she chose such a life of hardship never was, and never will be known."

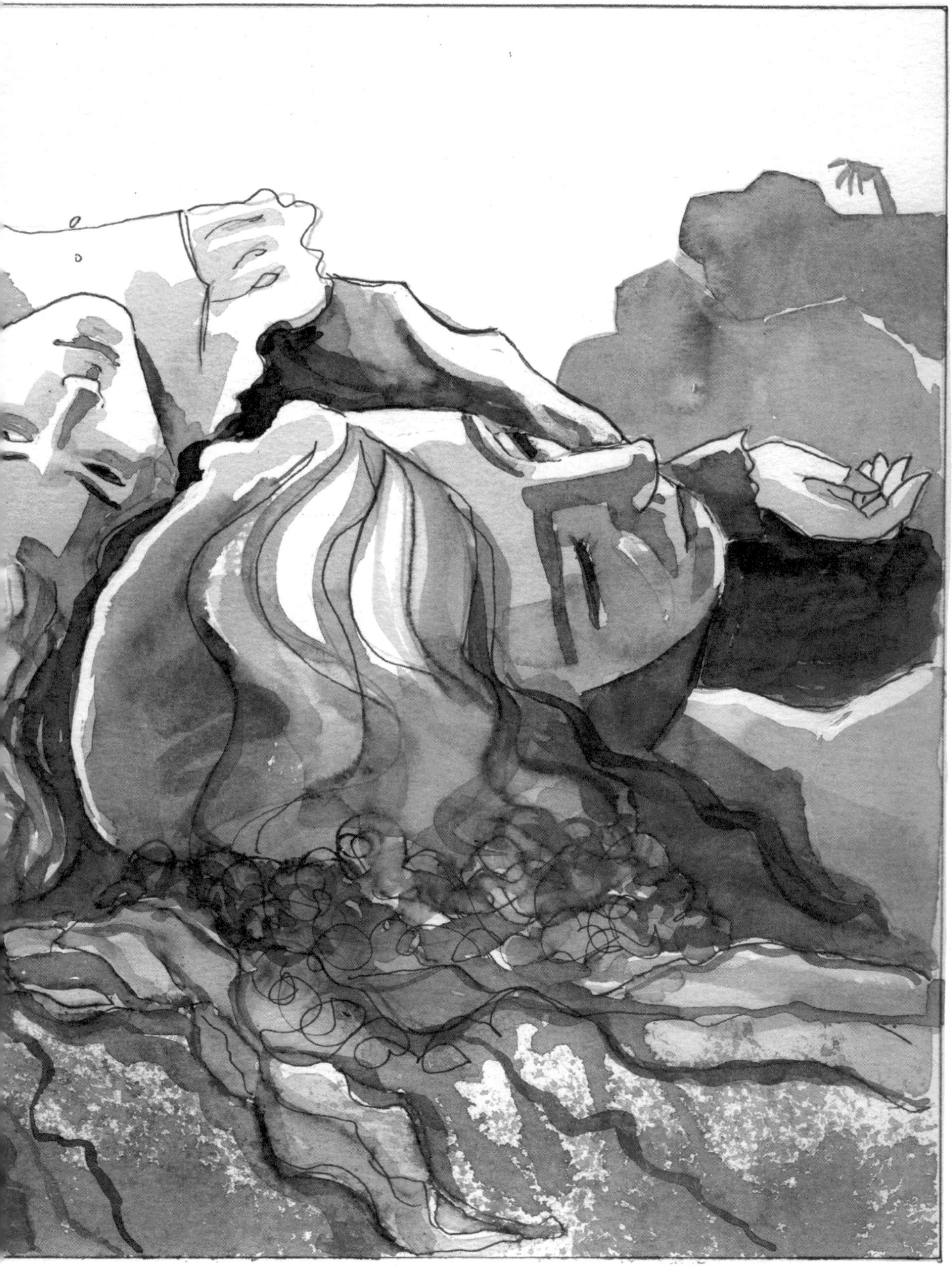

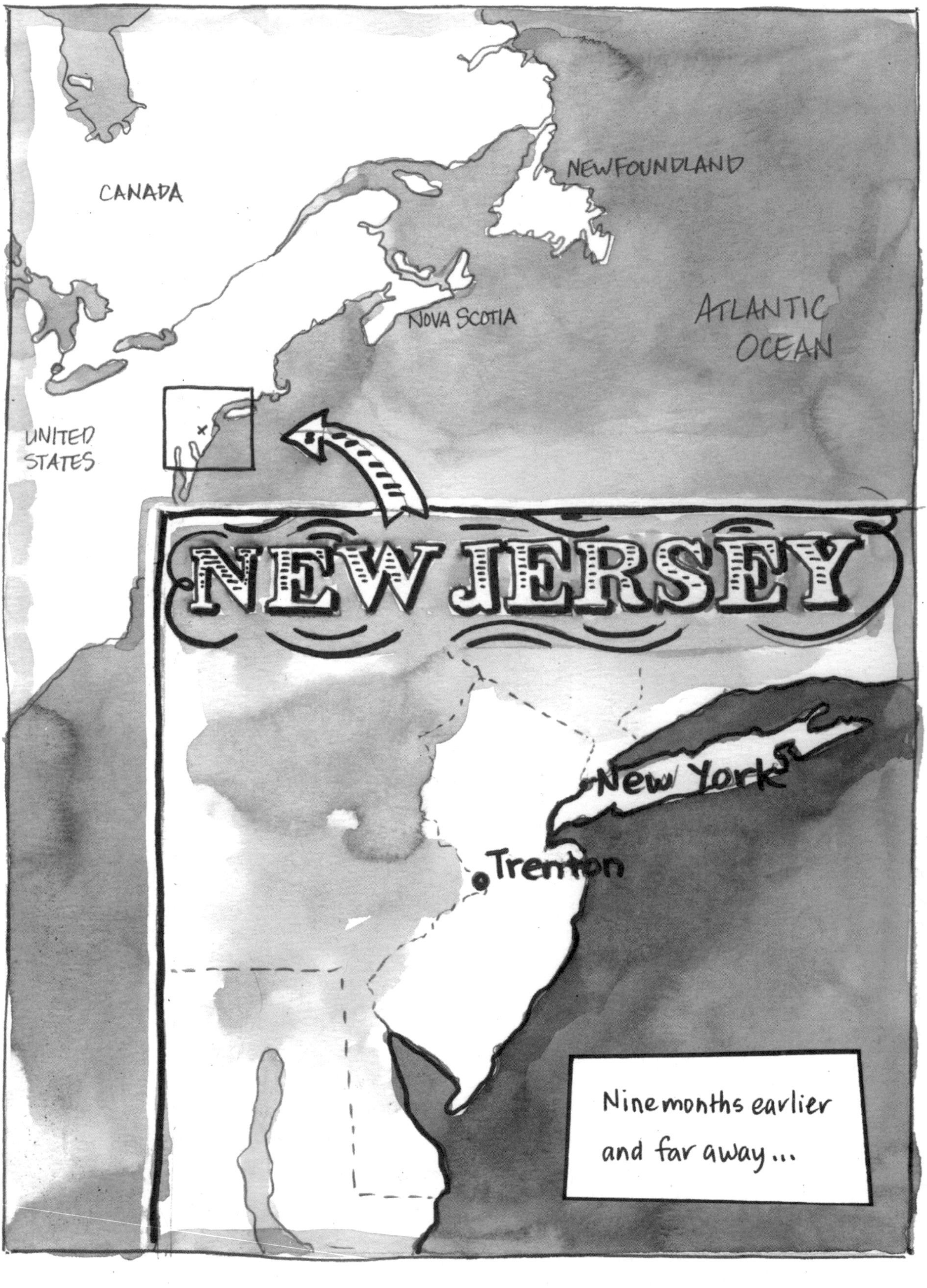
CANADA
NEWFOUNDLAND
NOVA SCOTIA
ATLANTIC OCEAN
UNITED STATES
NEW JERSEY
New York
Trenton
Nine months earlier and far away...

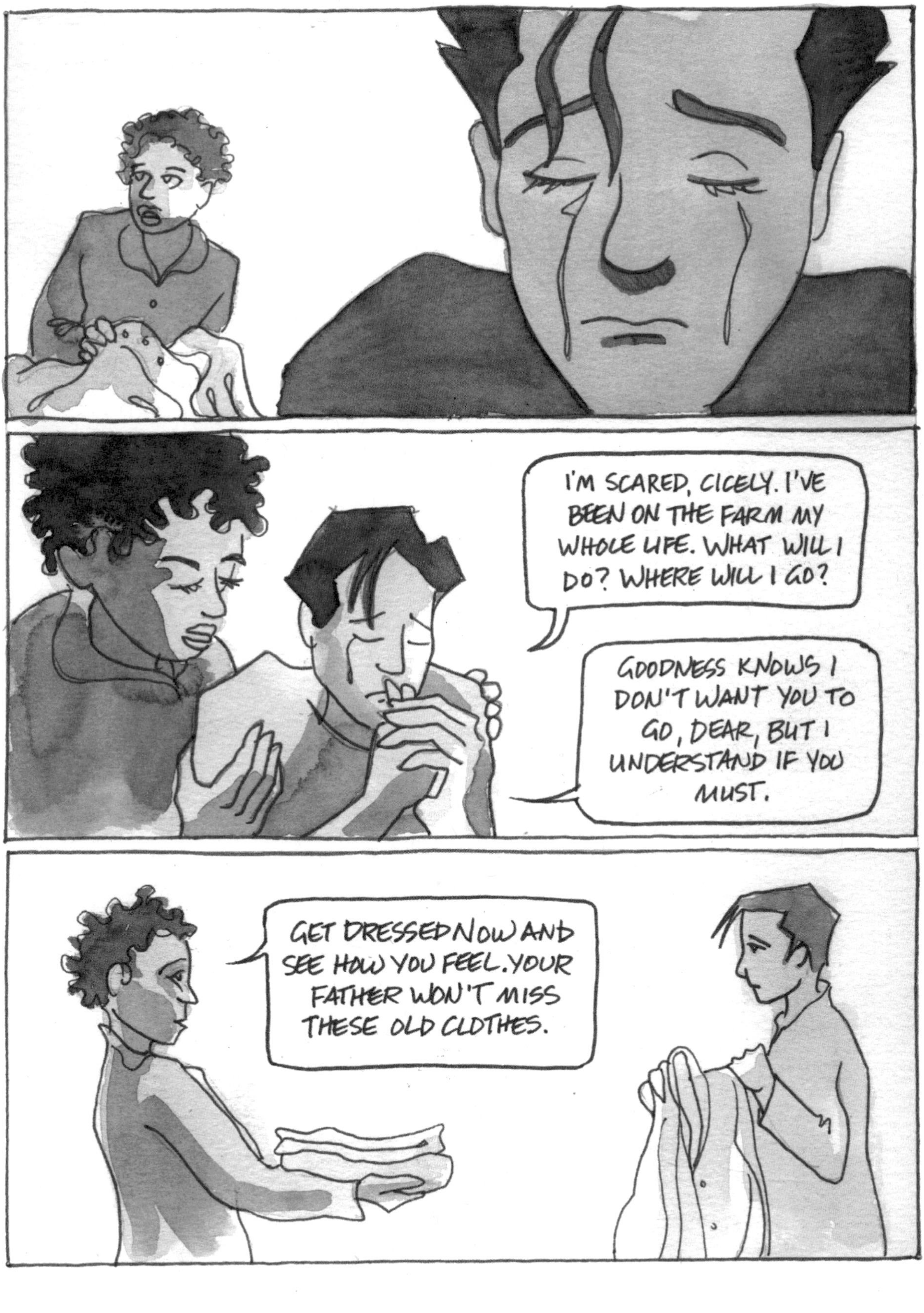
I'M SCARED, CICELY. I'VE BEEN ON THE FARM MY WHOLE LIFE. WHAT WILL I DO? WHERE WILL I GO?
GOODNESS KNOWS I DON'T WANT YOU TO GO, DEAR, BUT I UNDERSTAND IF YOU MUST.
GET DRESSED NOW AND SEE HOW YOU FEEL. YOUR FATHER WON'T MISS THESE OLD CLOTHES.

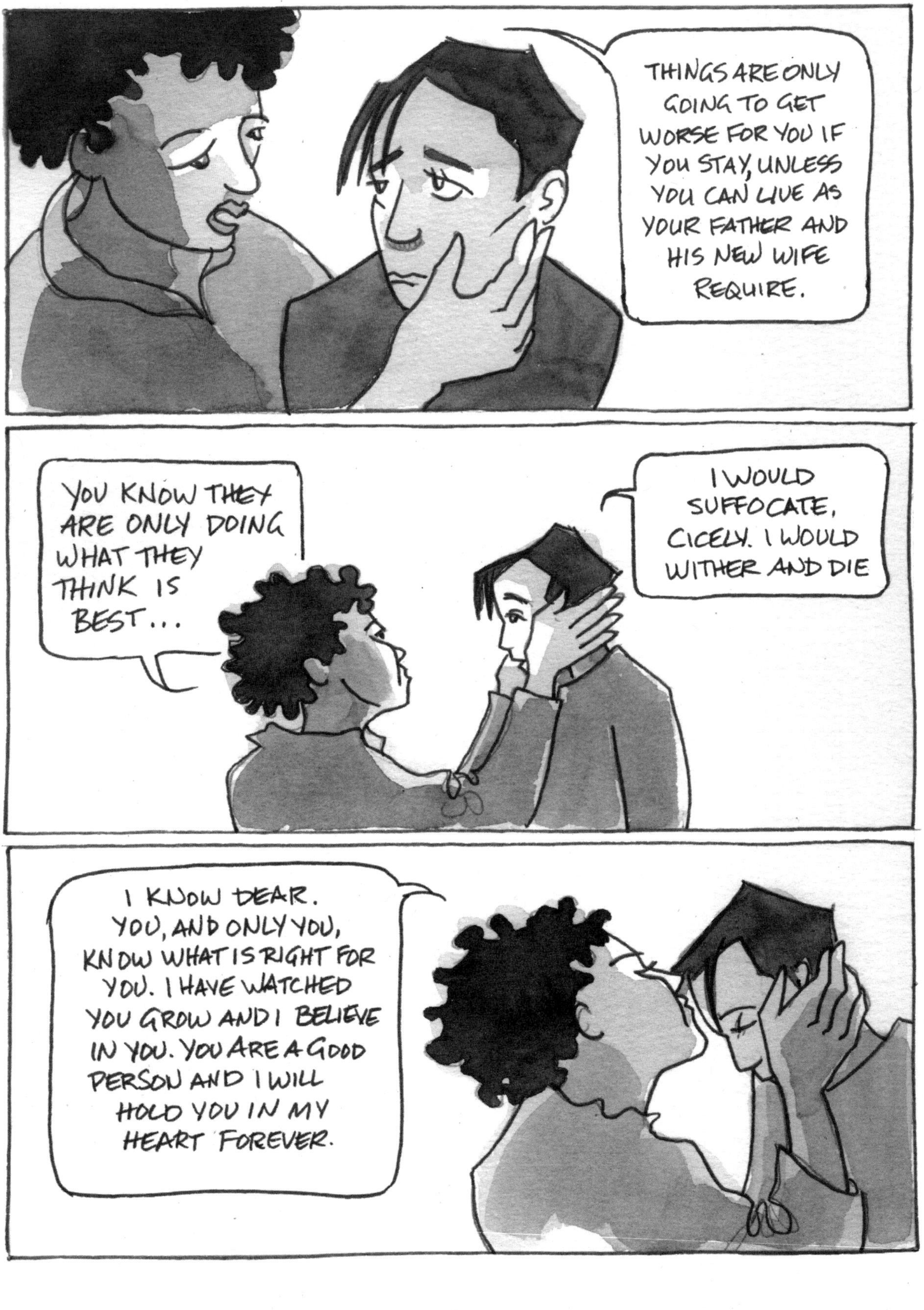
THINGS ARE ONLY GOING TO GET WORSE FOR YOU IF YOU STAY, UNLESS YOU CAN LIVE AS YOUR FATHER AND HIS NEW WIFE REQUIRE.
YOU KNOW THEY ARE ONLY DOING WHAT THEY THINK IS BEST...
I WOULD SUFFOCATE, CICELY. I WOULD WITHER AND DIE
I KNOW DEAR. YOU, AND ONLY YOU, KNOW WHAT IS RIGHT FOR YOU. I HAVE WATCHED YOU GROW AND I BELIEVE IN YOU. YOU ARE A GOOD PERSON AND I WILL HOLD YOU IN MY HEART FOREVER.

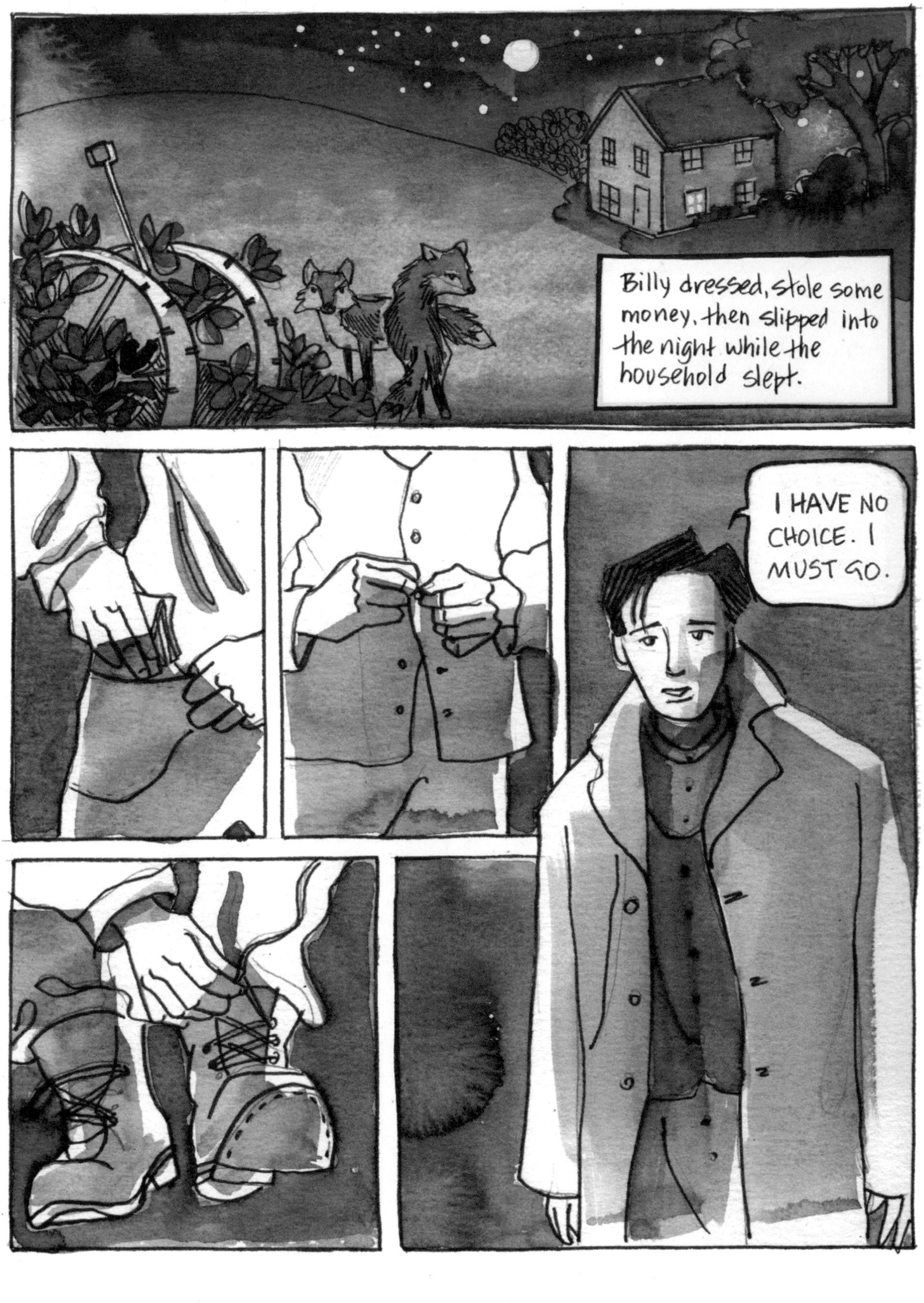
Billy dressed, stole some money, then slipped into the night while the household slept.
I HAVE NO CHOICE. I MUST GO.

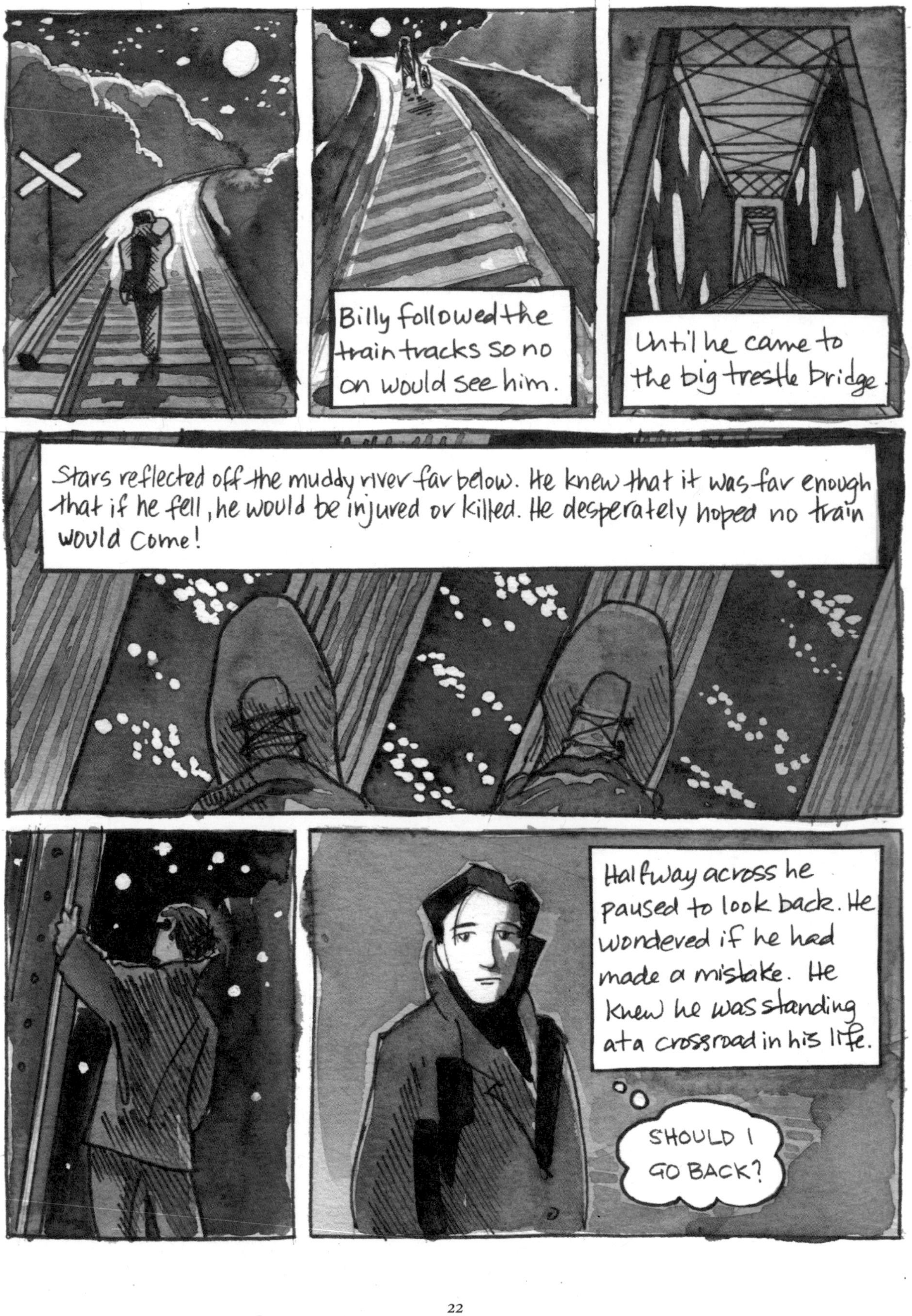
Billy followed the train tracks so no on would see him.
Until he came to the big trestle bridge.
Stars reflected off the muddy river far below. He knew that it was far enough that if he fell, he would be injured or killed. He desperately hoped no train would come!
Halfway across he paused to look back. He wondered if he had made a mistake. He knew he was standing at a crossroad in his life.
SHOULD I GO BACK?

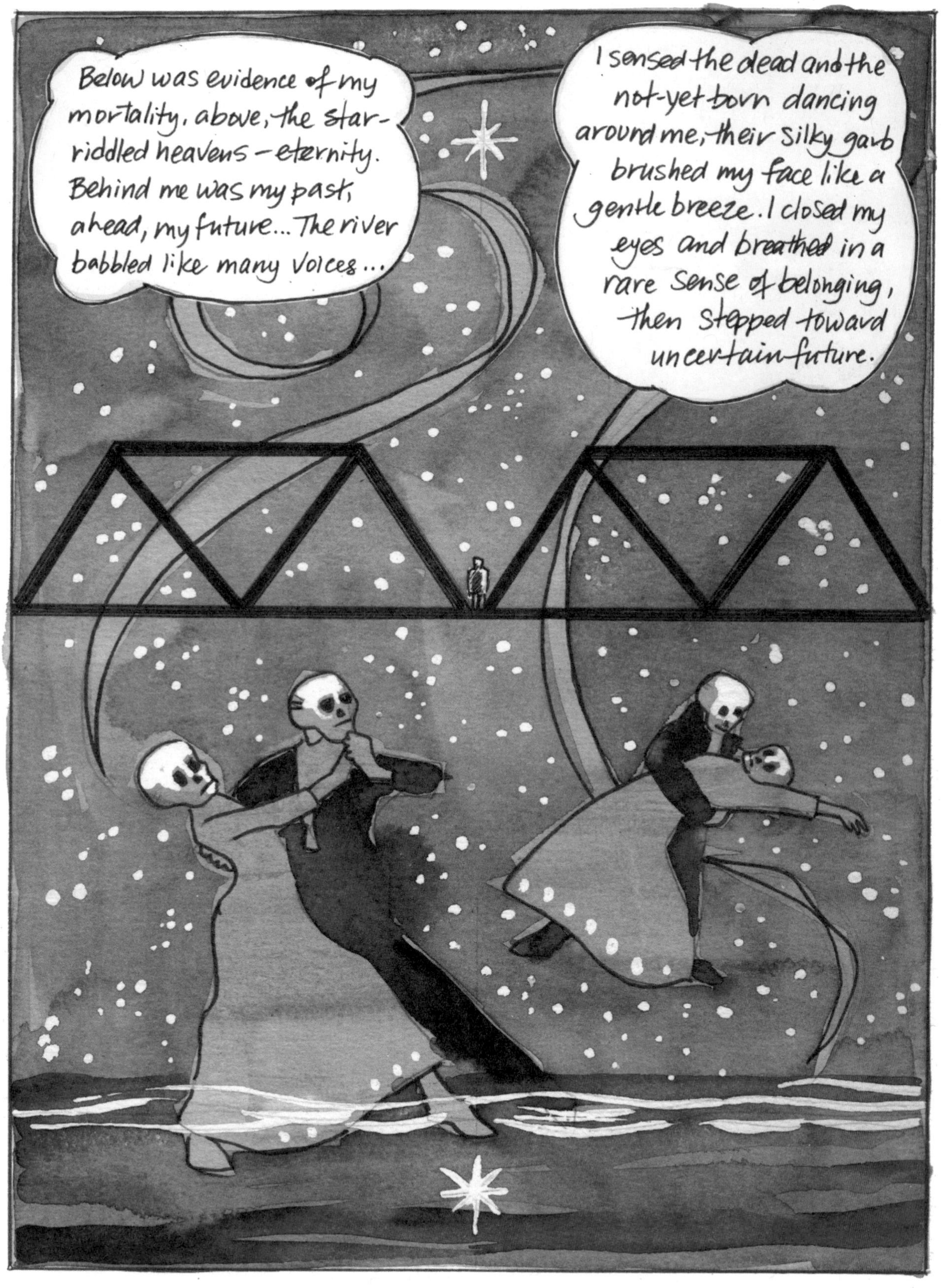
Below was evidence of my mortality, above, the star-riddled heavens – eternity. Behind me was my past, ahead, my future... The river babbled like many voices...
I sensed the dead and the not-yet born dancing around me, their silky garb brushed my face like a gentle breeze. I closed my eyes and breathed in a rare sense of belonging, then stepped toward uncertain future.

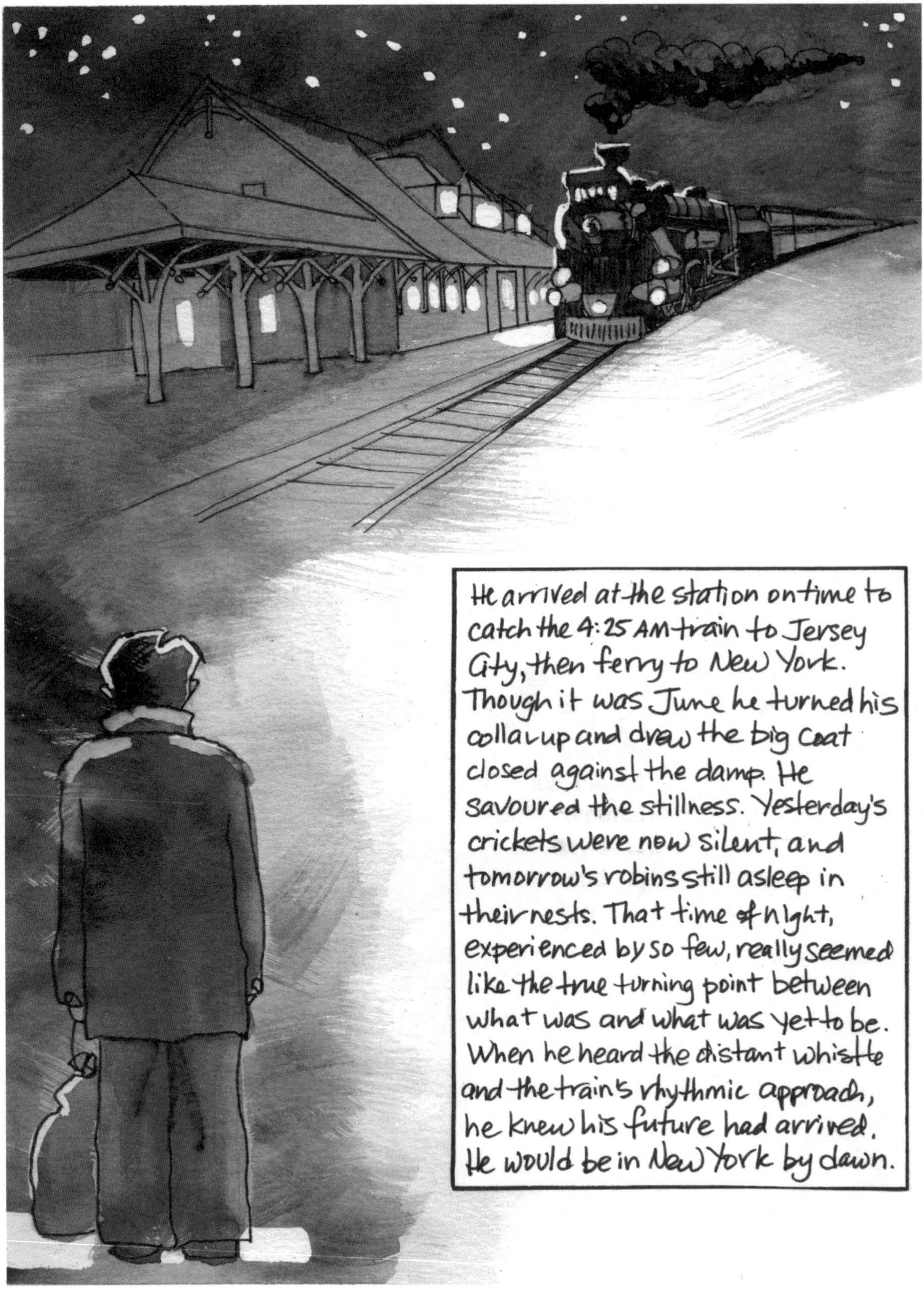
He arrived at the station on time to catch the 4:25 AM train to Jersey City, then ferry to New York. Though it was June he turned his collar up and drew the big coat closed against the damp. He savoured the stillness. Yesterday's crickets were now silent, and tomorrow's robins still asleep in their nests. That time of night, experienced by so few, really seemed like the true turning point between what was and what was yet to be. When he heard the distant whistle and the train's rhythmic approach, he knew his future had arrived. He would be in New York by dawn.

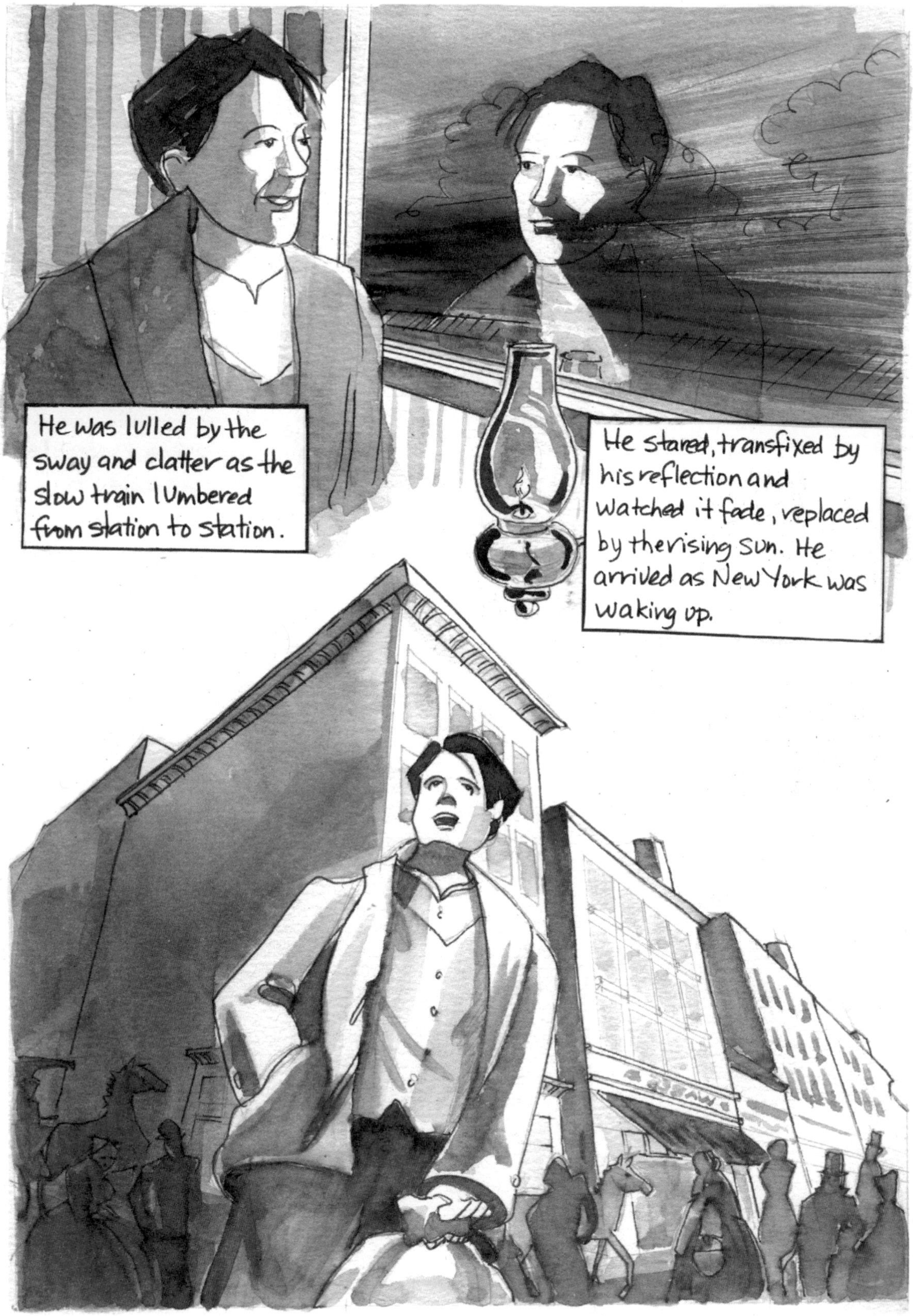
He was lulled by the sway and clatter as the slow train lumbered from station to station.
He stared, transfixed by his reflection and watched it fade, replaced by the rising sun. He arrived as New York was waking up.

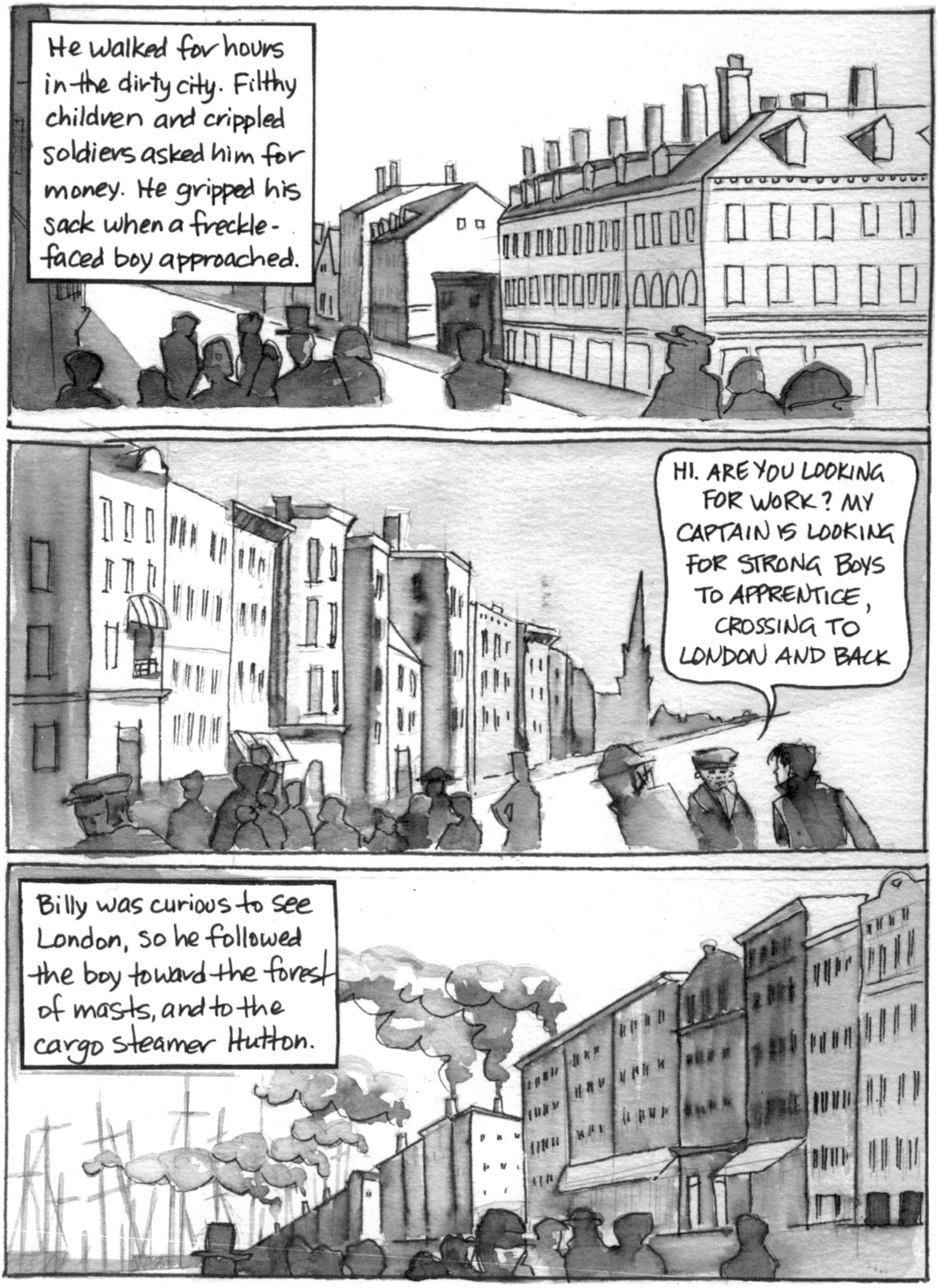
He walked for hours in the dirty city. Filthy children and crippled soldiers asked him for money. He gripped his sack when a freckle-faced boy approached.
HI. ARE YOU LOOKING FOR WORK? MY CAPTAIN IS LOOKING FOR STRONG BOYS TO APPRENTICE, CROSSING TO LONDON AND BACK
Billy was curious to see London, so he followed the boy toward the forest of masts, and to the cargo steamer Hutton.

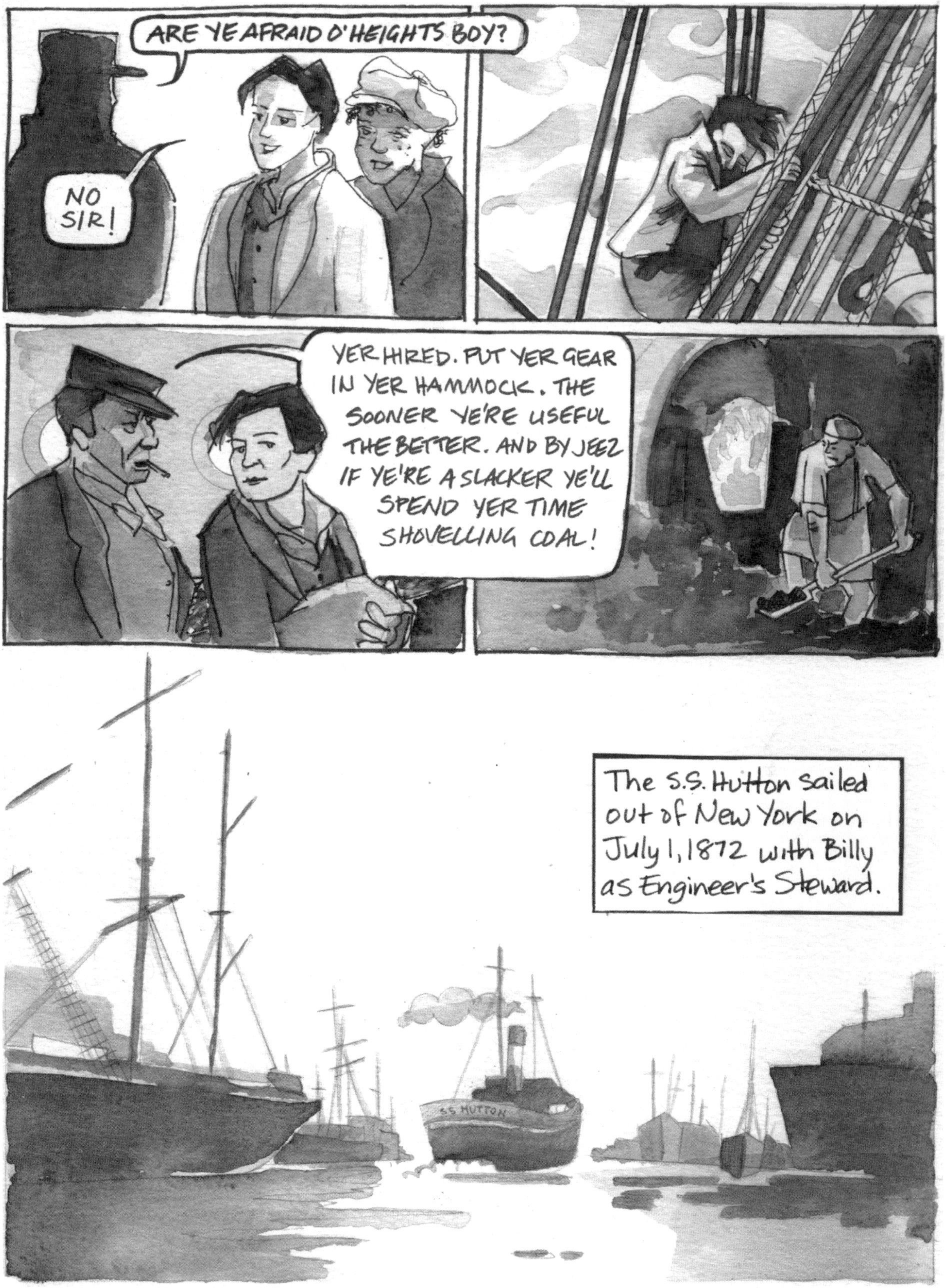
ARE YE AFRAID O' HEIGHTS BOY?
NO SIR!
YER HIRED. PUT YER GEAR IN YER HAMMOCK. THE SOONER YE'RE USEFUL THE BETTER. AND BY JEEZ IF YE'RE A SLACKER YE'LL SPEND YER TIME SHOVELLING COAL!
The S.S. Hutton sailed out of New York on July 1, 1872 with Billy as Engineer's Steward.
S.S. HUTTON

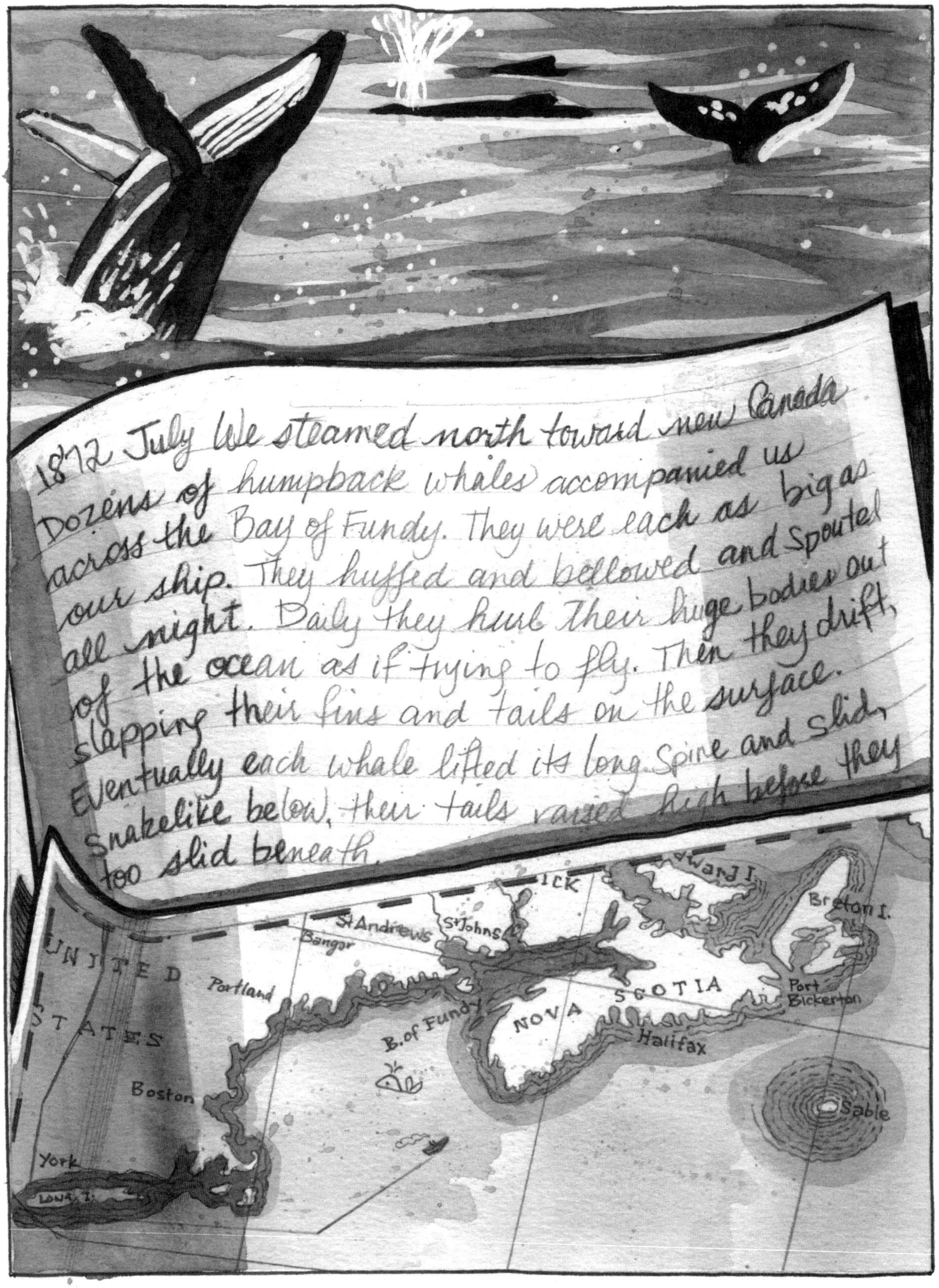
1872 July We steamed north toward new Canada
Dozens of humpback whales accompanied us
across the Bay of Fundy. They were each as big as
our ship. They huffed and bellowed and spouted
all night. Daily they hurl their huge bodies out
of the ocean as if trying to fly. Then they drift,
slapping their fins and tails on the surface.
Eventually each whale lifted its long spine and slid,
snakelike below, their tails raised high before they
too slid beneath.
St Andrews
St Johns
Bangor
Breton I.
UNITED
STATES
Portland
NOVA SCOTIA
Port Bickerton
B. of Fundy
Halifax
Boston
Sable
York
LONG I.

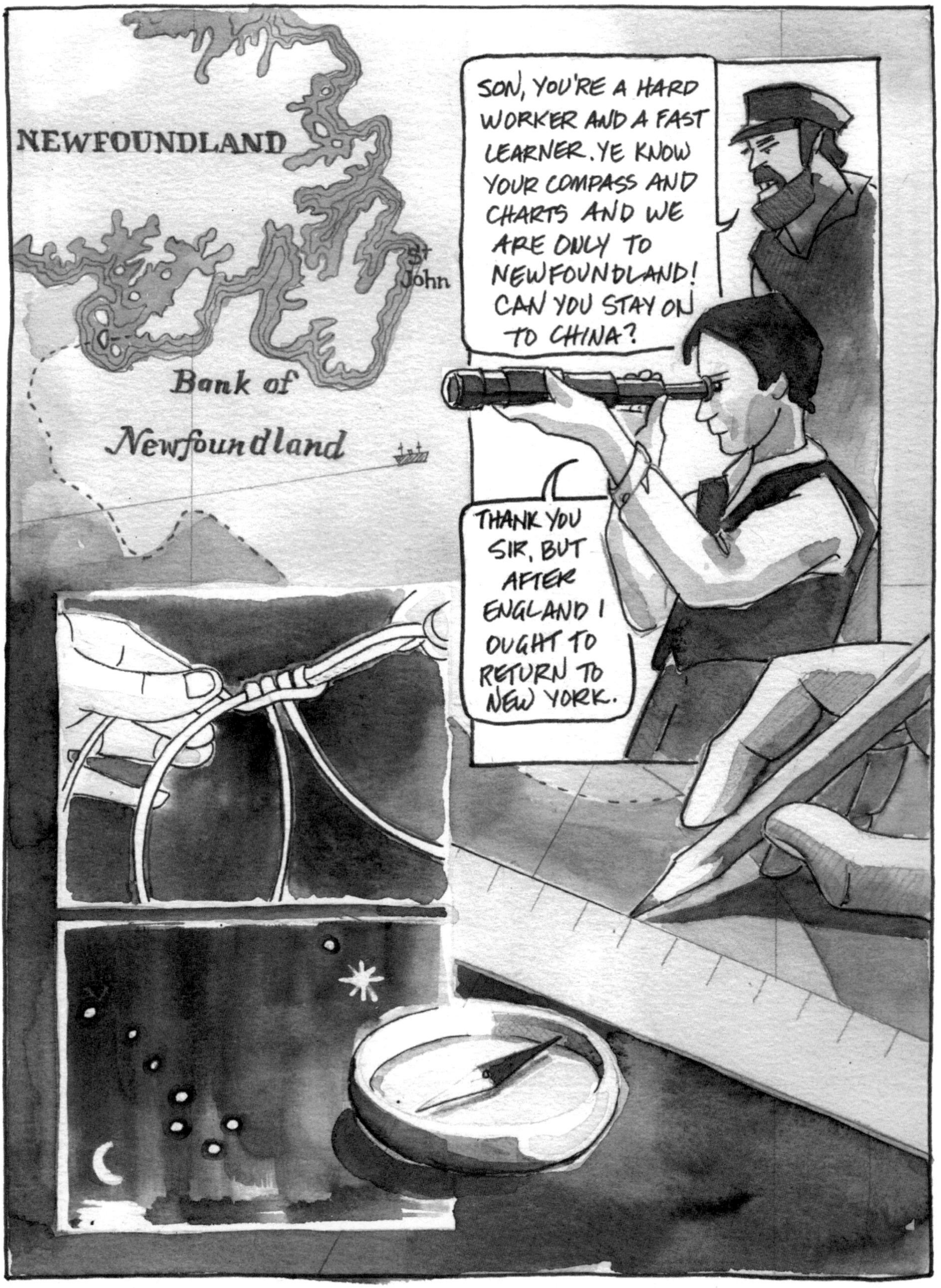
NEWFOUNDLAND
St John
Bank of
Newfoundland
SON, YOU'RE A HARD WORKER AND A FAST LEARNER. YE KNOW YOUR COMPASS AND CHARTS AND WE ARE ONLY TO NEWFOUNDLAND! CAN YOU STAY ON TO CHINA?
THANK YOU SIR, BUT AFTER ENGLAND I OUGHT TO RETURN TO NEW YORK.

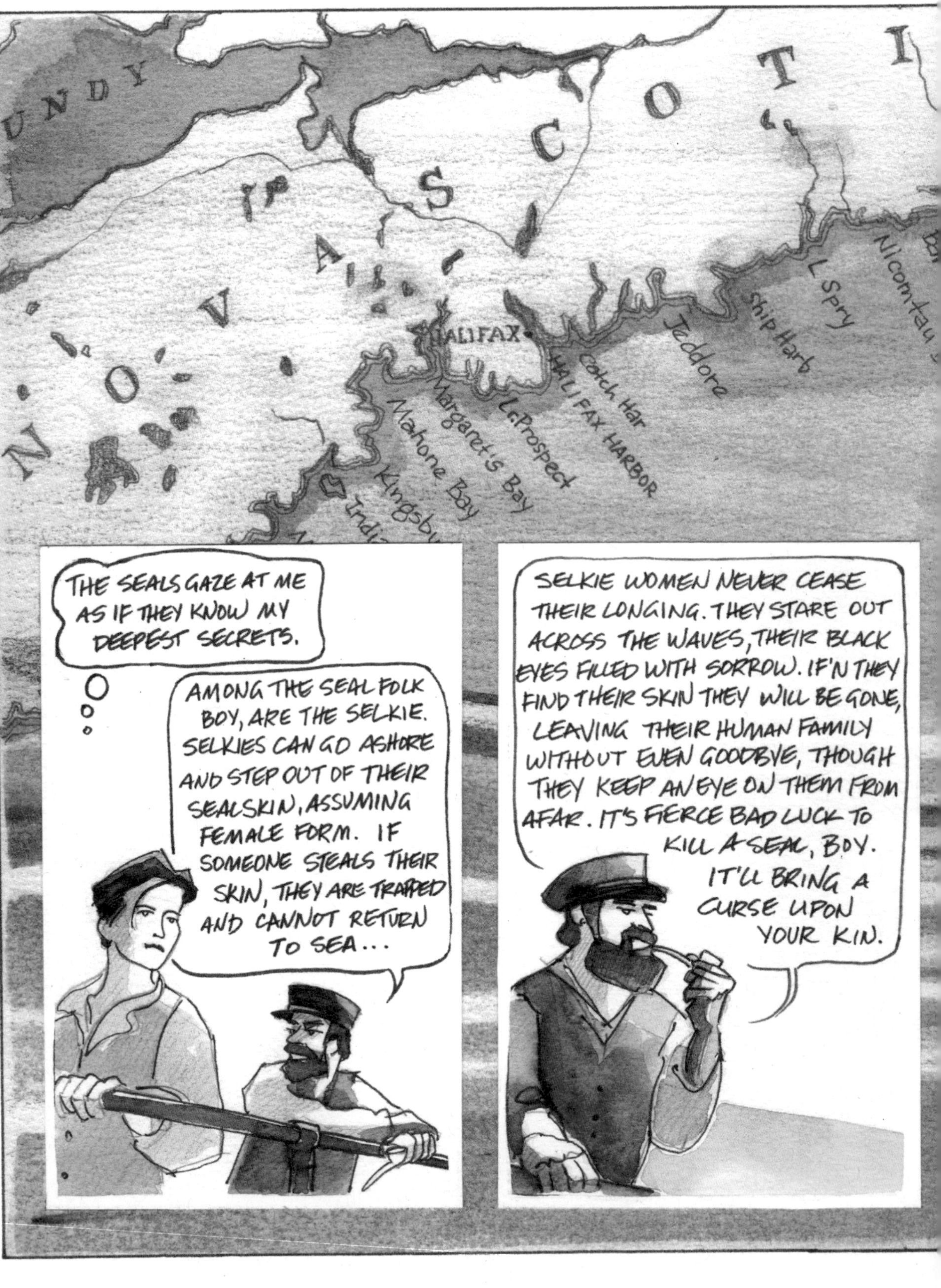
UNDY
NOVA SCOTI
HALIFAX
Margaret's Bay
Mahone Bay
Lt.Prospect
HALIFAX HARBOR
Cotch Har
Jeddore
Ship Harb
L Spry
Nicomtau
THE SEALS GAZE AT ME AS IF THEY KNOW MY DEEPEST SECRETS.
AMONG THE SEAL FOLK BOY, ARE THE SELKIE. SELKIES CAN GO ASHORE AND STEP OUT OF THEIR SEALSKIN, ASSUMING FEMALE FORM. IF SOMEONE STEALS THEIR SKIN, THEY ARE TRAPPED AND CANNOT RETURN TO SEA...
SELKIE WOMEN NEVER CEASE THEIR LONGING. THEY STARE OUT ACROSS THE WAVES, THEIR BLACK EYES FILLED WITH SORROW. IF'N THEY FIND THEIR SKIN THEY WILL BE GONE, LEAVING THEIR HUMAN FAMILY WITHOUT EVEN GOODBYE, THOUGH THEY KEEP AN EYE ON THEM FROM AFAR. IT'S FIERCE BAD LUCK TO KILL A SEAL, BOY.
IT'LL BRING A CURSE UPON YOUR KIN.

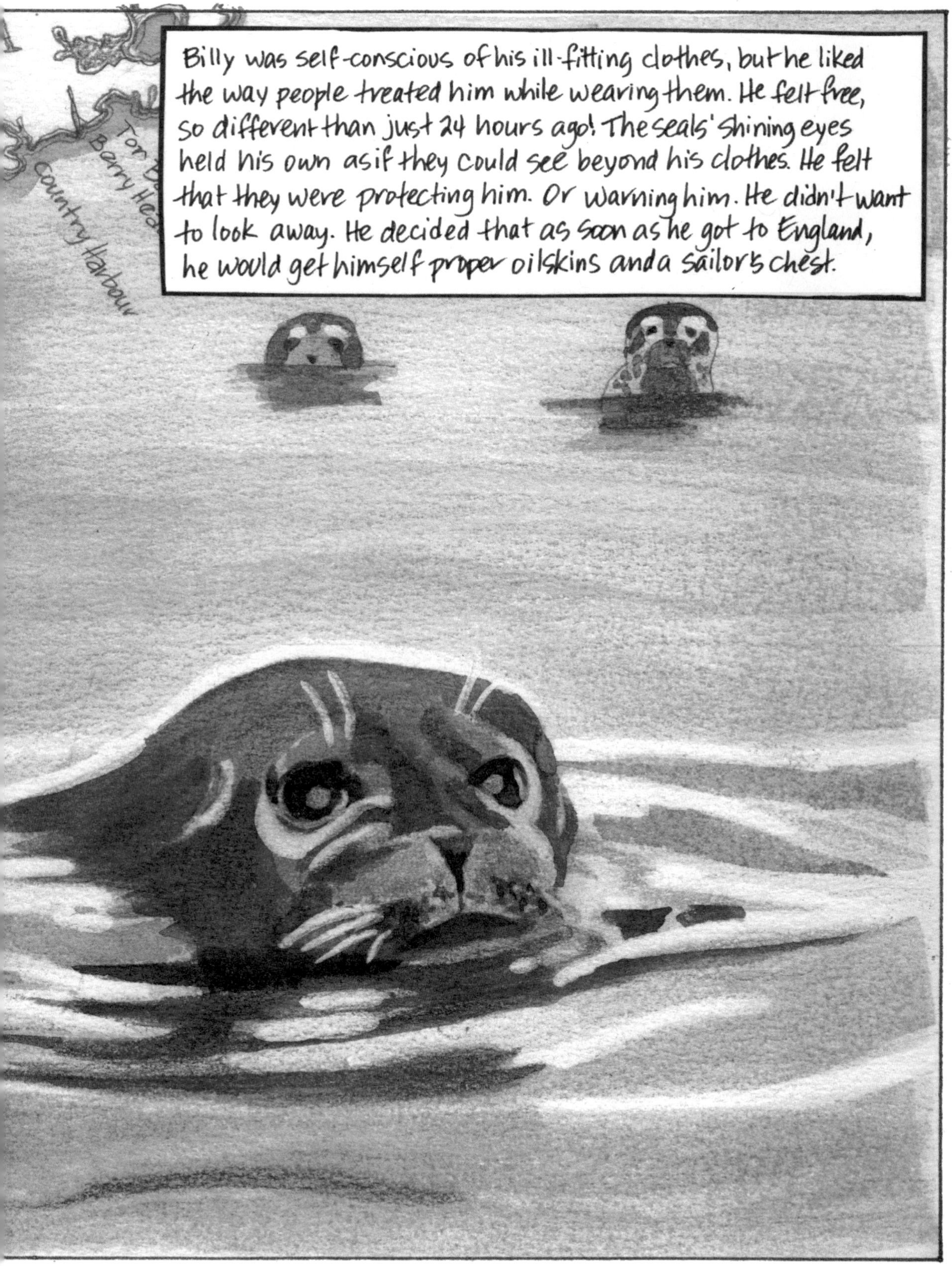
Billy was self-conscious of his ill-fitting clothes, but he liked the way people treated him while wearing them. He felt free, so different than just 24 hours ago! The seals' shining eyes held his own as if they could see beyond his clothes. He felt that they were protecting him. Or warning him. He didn't want to look away. He decided that as soon as he got to England, he would get himself proper oilskins and a sailor's chest.
Country Harbour

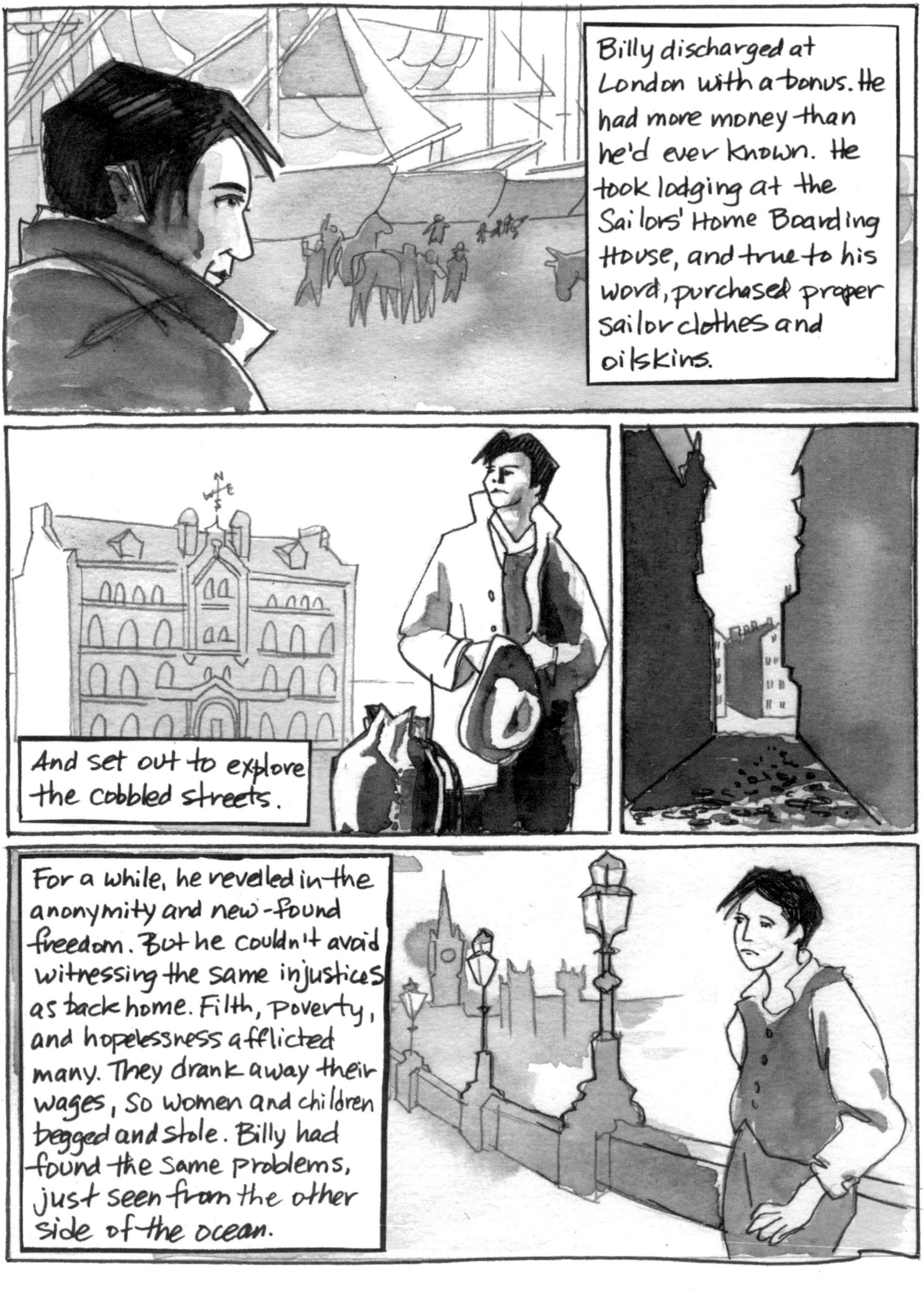
Billy discharged at London with a bonus. He had more money than he'd ever known. He took lodging at the Sailors' Home Boarding House, and true to his word, purchased proper sailor clothes and oilskins.
And set out to explore the cobbled streets.
For a while, he revelled in the anonymity and new-found freedom. But he couldn't avoid witnessing the same injustices as back home. Filth, poverty, and hopelessness afflicted many. They drank away their wages, so women and children begged and stole. Billy had found the same problems, just seen from the other side of the ocean.

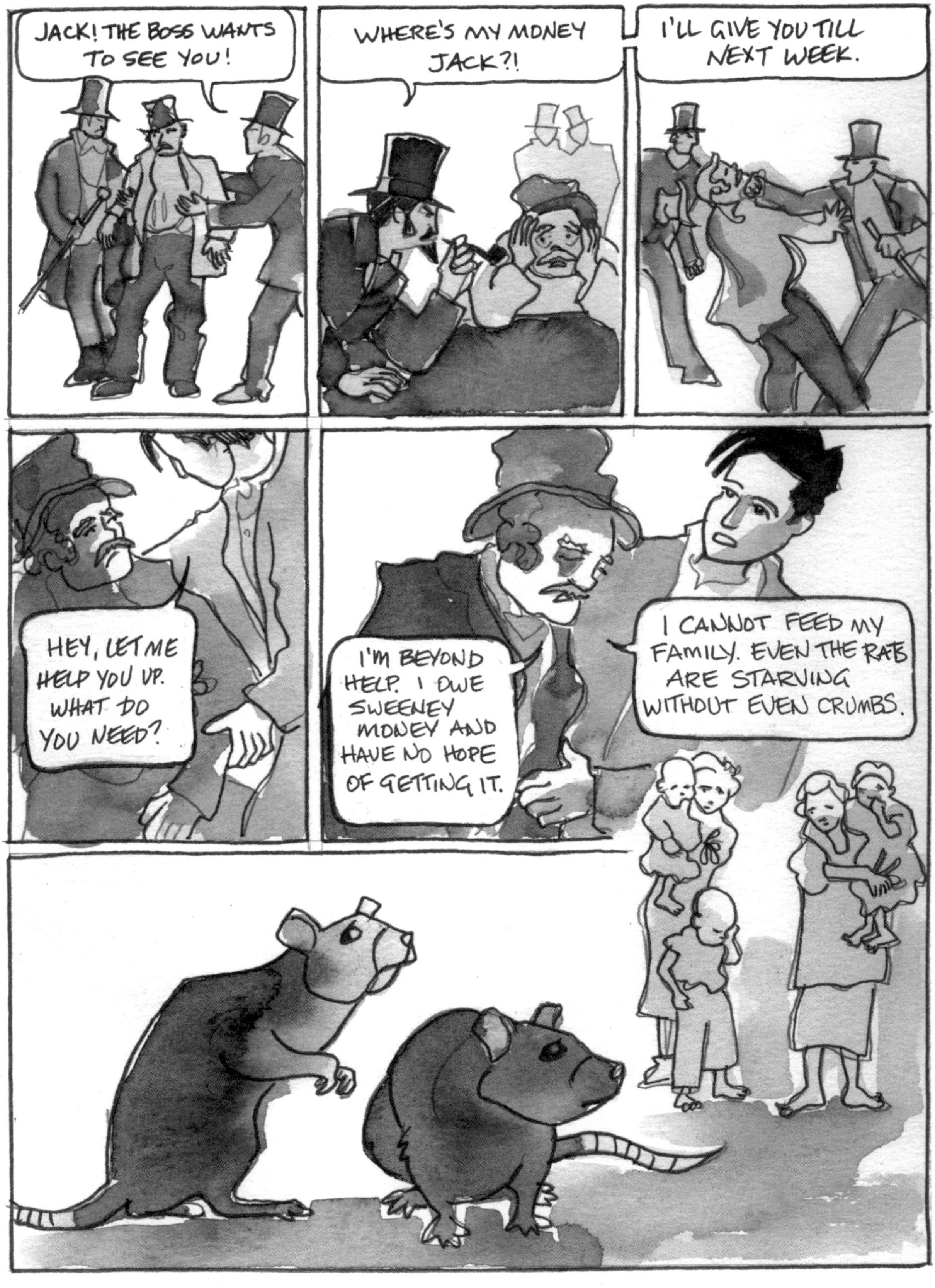
JACK! THE BOSS WANTS TO SEE YOU!
WHERE'S MY MONEY JACK?!
I'LL GIVE YOU TILL NEXT WEEK.
HEY, LET ME HELP YOU UP. WHAT DO YOU NEED?
I'M BEYOND HELP. I OWE SWEENEY MONEY AND HAVE NO HOPE OF GETTING IT.
I CANNOT FEED MY FAMILY. EVEN THE RATS ARE STARVING WITHOUT EVEN CRUMBS.

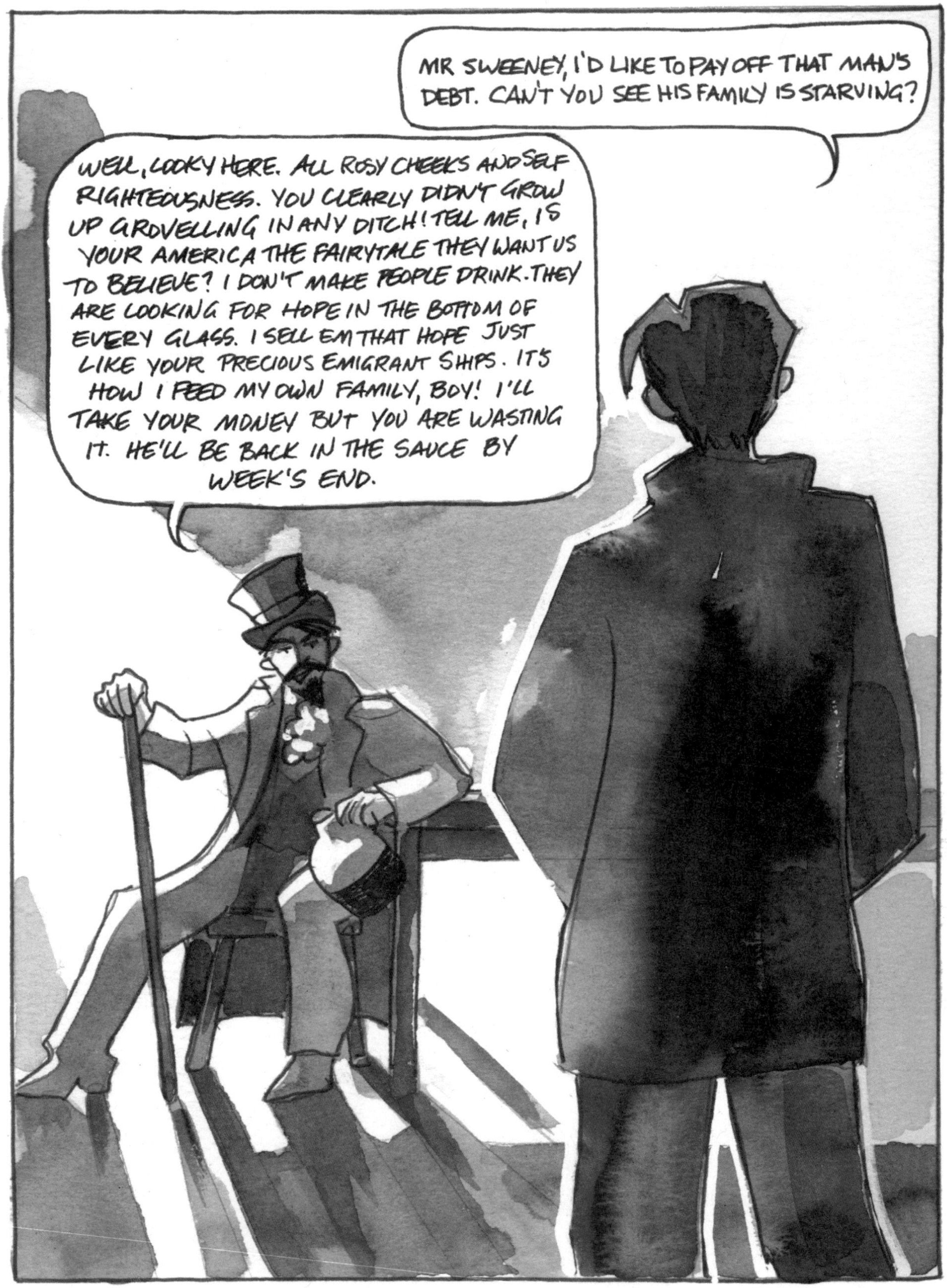
MR SWEENEY, I'D LIKE TO PAY OFF THAT MAN'S DEBT. CAN'T YOU SEE HIS FAMILY IS STARVING?
WELL, LOOKY HERE. ALL ROSY CHEEKS AND SELF RIGHTEOUSNESS. YOU CLEARLY DIDN'T GROW UP GROVELLING IN ANY DITCH! TELL ME, IS YOUR AMERICA THE FAIRYTALE THEY WANT US TO BELIEVE? I DON'T MAKE PEOPLE DRINK. THEY ARE LOOKING FOR HOPE IN THE BOTTOM OF EVERY GLASS. I SELL EM THAT HOPE JUST LIKE YOUR PRECIOUS EMIGRANT SHIPS. IT'S HOW I FEED MY OWN FAMILY, BOY! I'LL TAKE YOUR MONEY BUT YOU ARE WASTING IT. HE'LL BE BACK IN THE SAUCE BY WEEK'S END.

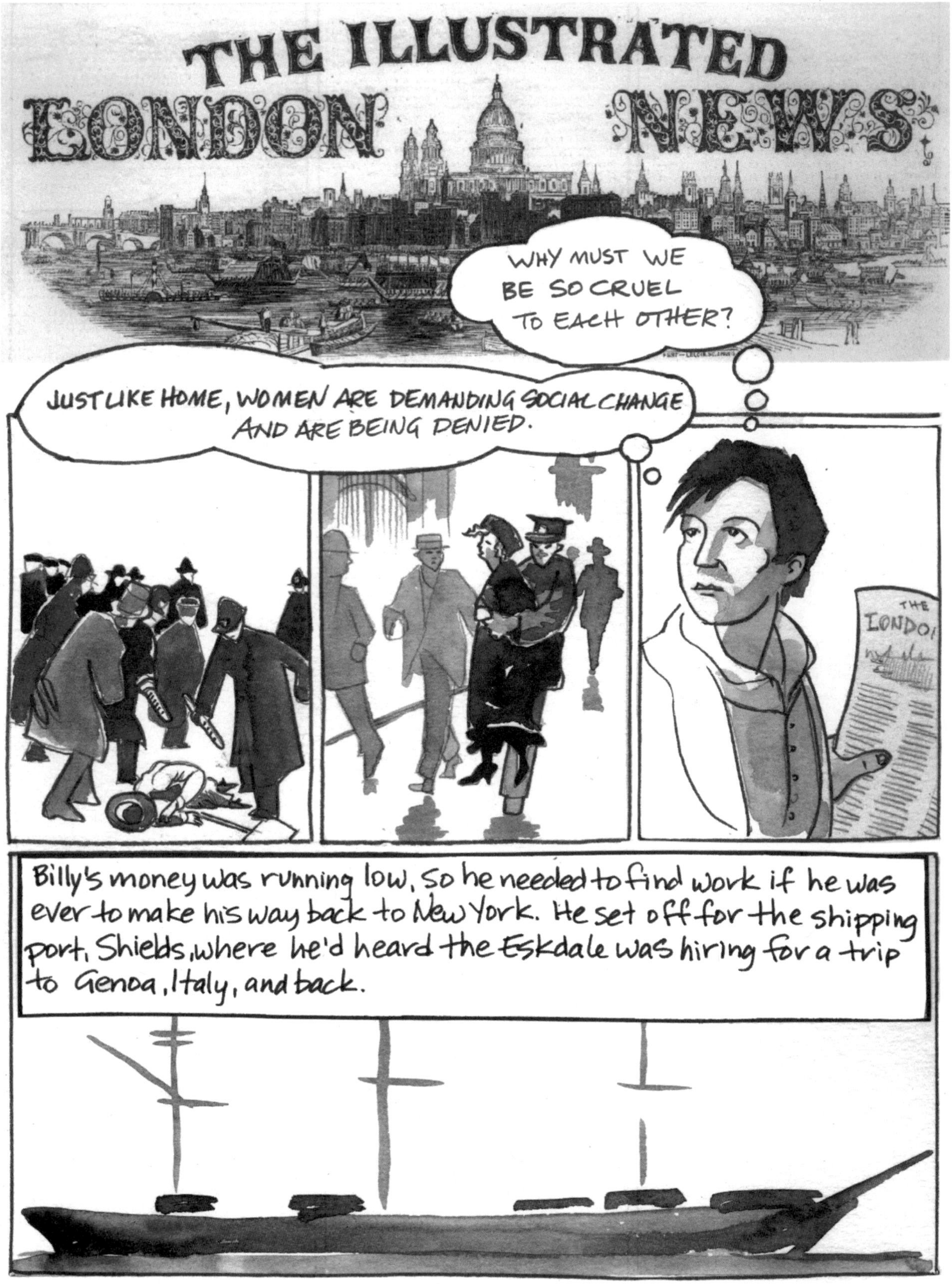
THE ILLUSTRATED LONDON NEWS
WHY MUST WE BE SO CRUEL TO EACH OTHER?
JUST LIKE HOME, WOMEN ARE DEMANDING SOCIAL CHANGE AND ARE BEING DENIED.
THE LONDO
Billy's money was running low, so he needed to find work if he was ever to make his way back to New York. He set off for the shipping port, Shields, where he'd heard the Eskdale was hiring for a trip to Genoa, Italy, and back.

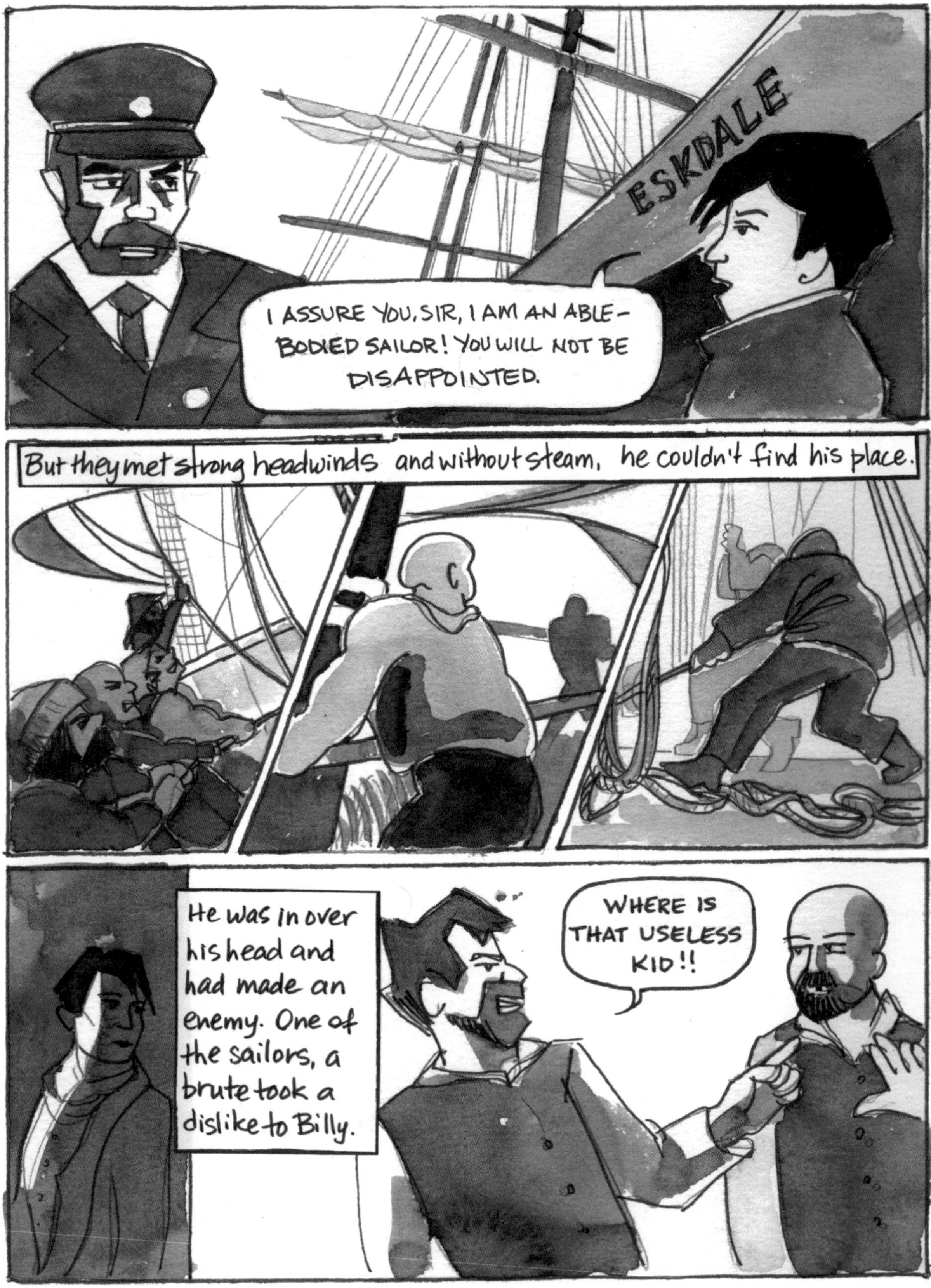
ESKDALE
I ASSURE YOU, SIR, I AM AN ABLE-BODIED SAILOR! YOU WILL NOT BE DISAPPOINTED.
But they met strong headwinds and without steam, he couldn't find his place.
He was in over his head and had made an enemy. One of the sailors, a brute took a dislike to Billy.
WHERE IS THAT USELESS KID!!

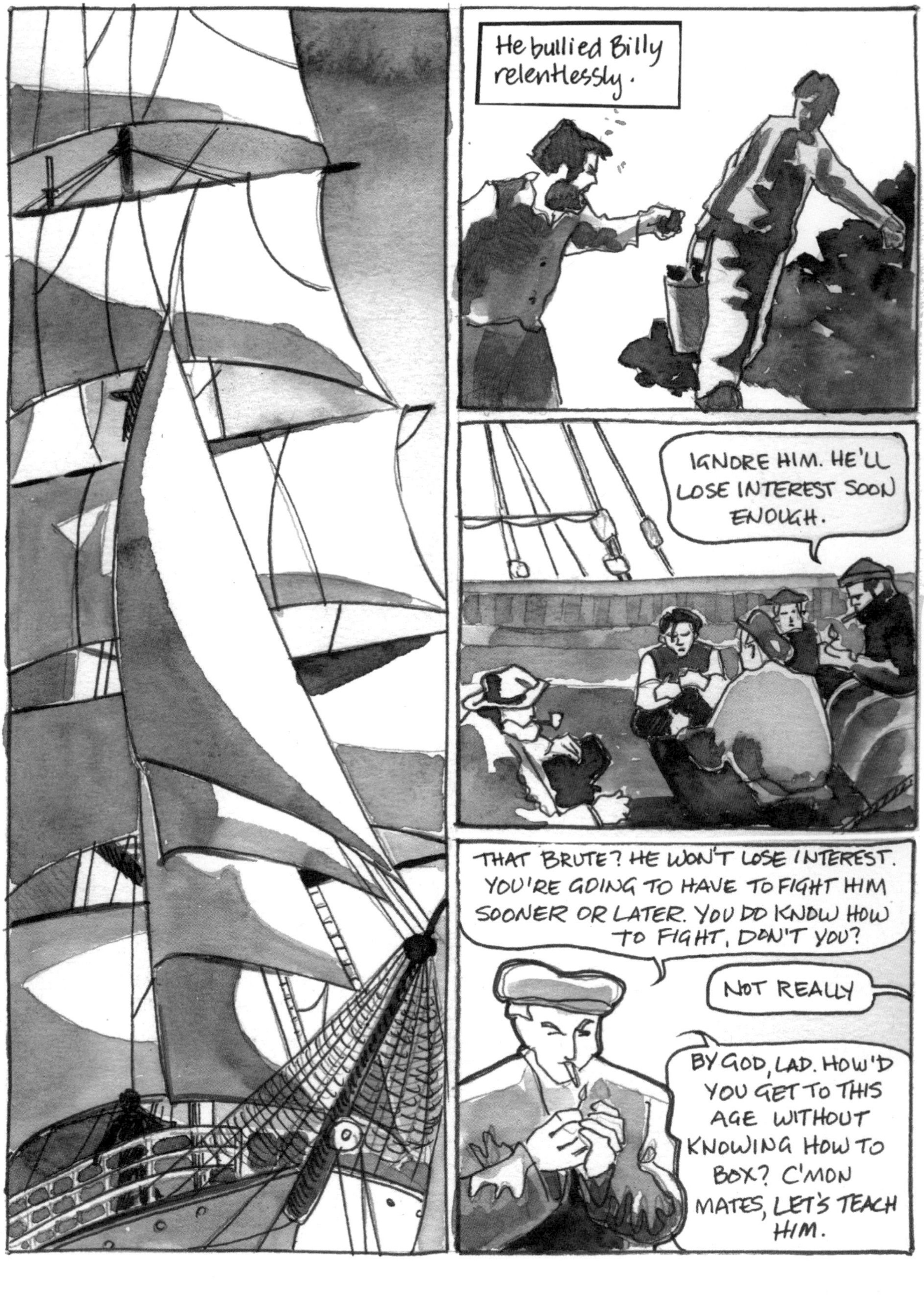

He bullied Billy relentlessly.
IGNORE HIM. HE'LL LOSE INTEREST SOON ENOUGH.
THAT BRUTE? HE WON'T LOSE INTEREST. YOU'RE GOING TO HAVE TO FIGHT HIM SOONER OR LATER. YOU DO KNOW HOW TO FIGHT, DON'T YOU?
NOT REALLY
BY GOD, LAD. HOW'D YOU GET TO THIS AGE WITHOUT KNOWING HOW TO BOX? C'MON MATES, LET'S TEACH HIM.

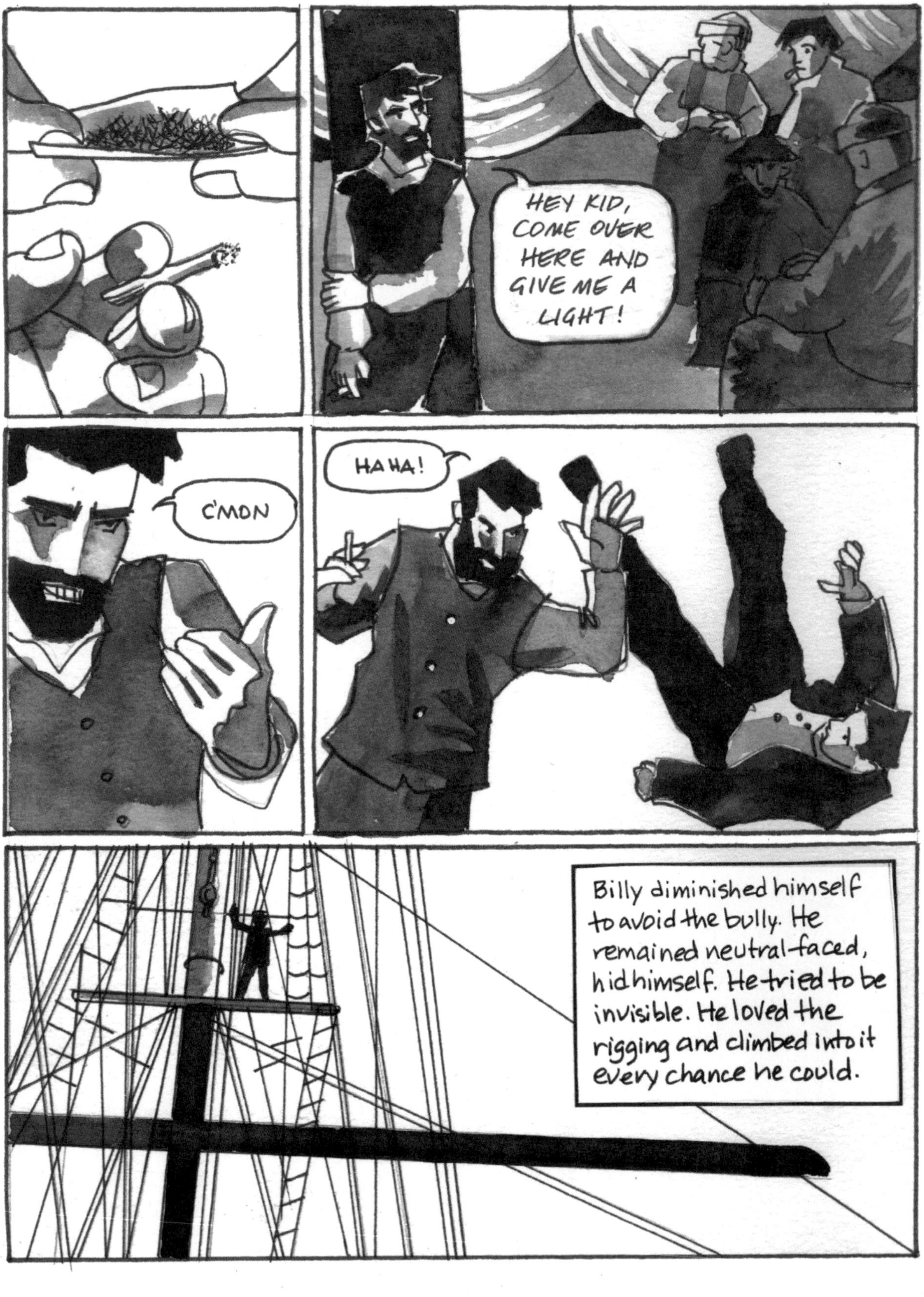
HEY KID, COME OVER HERE AND GIVE ME A LIGHT!
C'MON
HAHA!
Billy diminished himself to avoid the bully. He remained neutral-faced, hid himself. He tried to be invisible. He loved the rigging and climbed into it every chance he could.

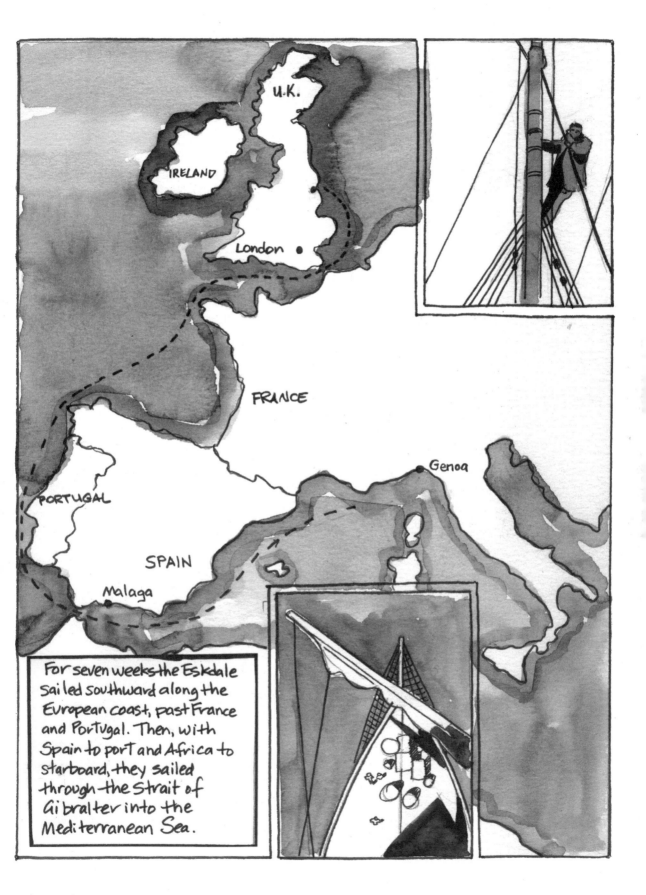

U.K.

IRELAND

London

FRANCE

Genoa

PORTUGAL

SPAIN

Malaga

For seven weeks the Eskdale
sailed southward along the
European coast, past France
and Portugal. Then, with
Spain to port and Africa to
starboard, they sailed
through the Strait of
Gibralter into the
Mediterranean Sea.

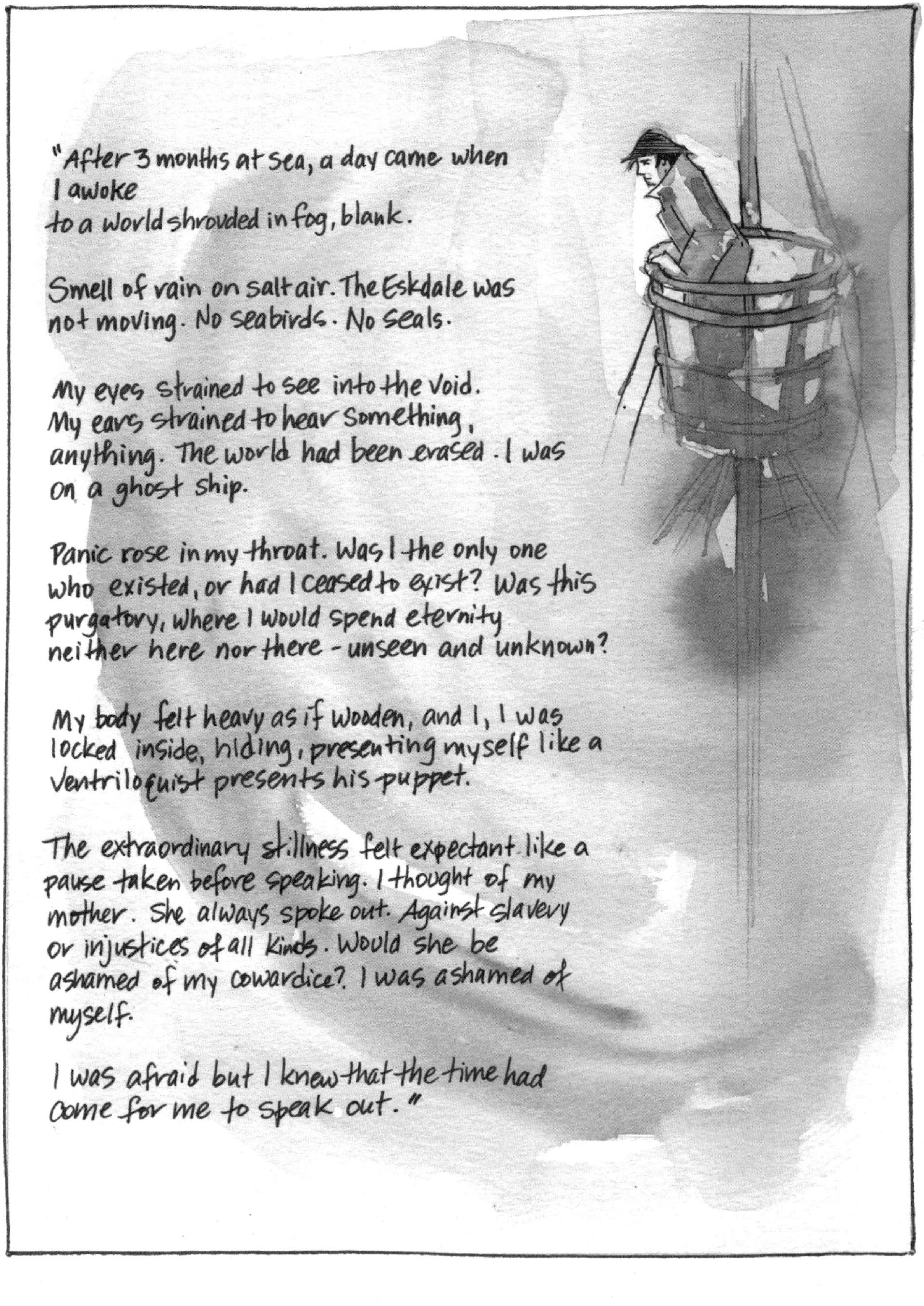
"After 3 months at sea, a day came when I awoke to a world shrouded in fog, blank.
Smell of rain on salt air. The Eskdale was not moving. No seabirds. No seals.
My eyes strained to see into the void. My ears strained to hear something, anything. The world had been erased. I was on a ghost ship.
Panic rose in my throat. Was I the only one who existed, or had I ceased to exist? Was this purgatory, where I would spend eternity neither here nor there - unseen and unknown?
My body felt heavy as if wooden, and I, I was locked inside, hiding, presenting myself like a ventriloquist presents his puppet.
The extraordinary stillness felt expectant like a pause taken before speaking. I thought of my mother. She always spoke out. Against slavery or injustices of all kinds. Would she be ashamed of my cowardice? I was ashamed of myself.
I was afraid but I knew that the time had come for me to speak out."

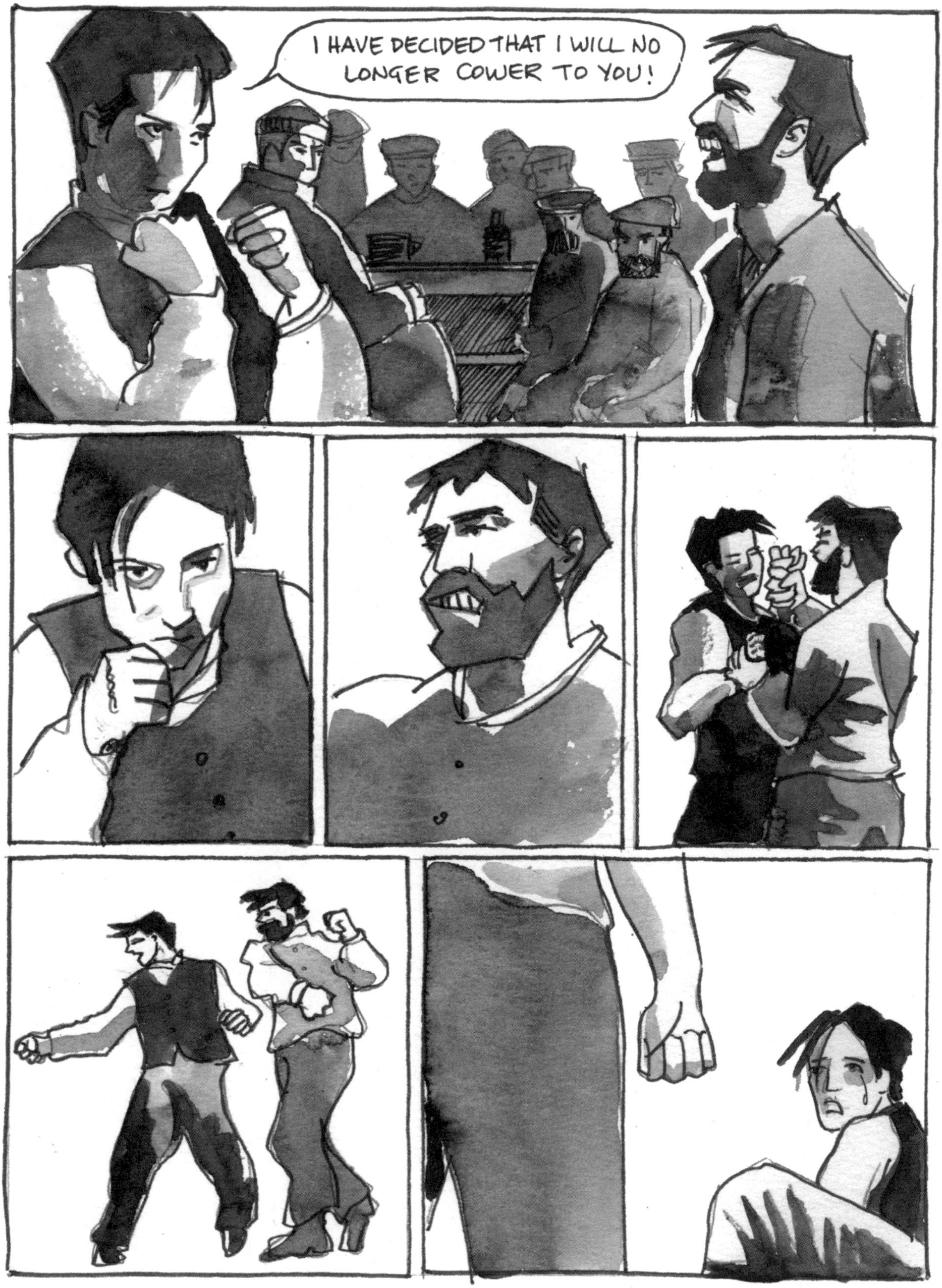
I HAVE DECIDED THAT I WILL NO LONGER COWER TO YOU!

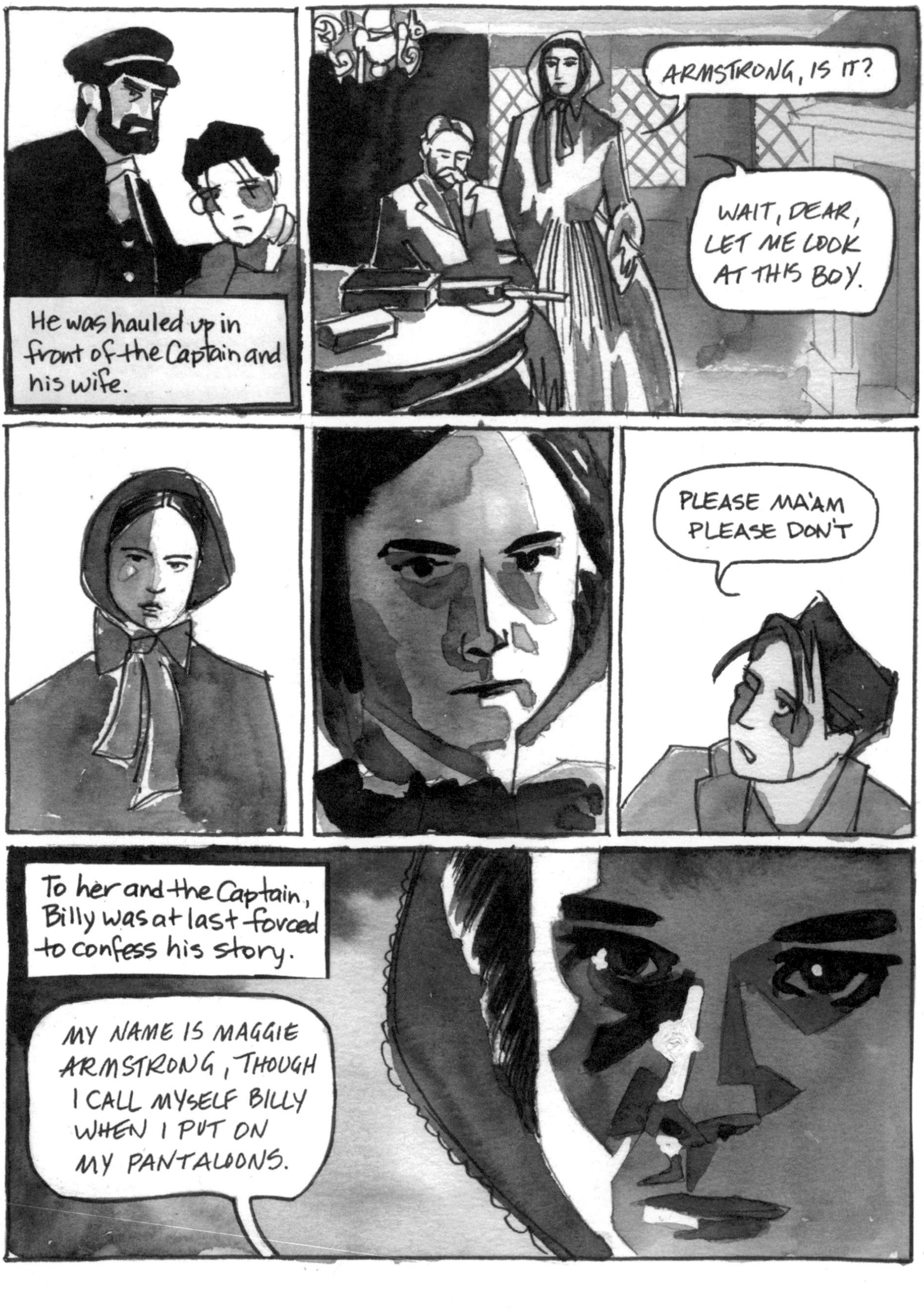
He was hauled up in front of the Captain and his wife.
ARMSTRONG, IS IT?
WAIT, DEAR, LET ME LOOK AT THIS BOY.
PLEASE MA'AM PLEASE DON'T
To her and the Captain, Billy was at last forced to confess his story.
MY NAME IS MAGGIE ARMSTRONG, THOUGH I CALL MYSELF BILLY WHEN I PUT ON MY PANTALOONS.

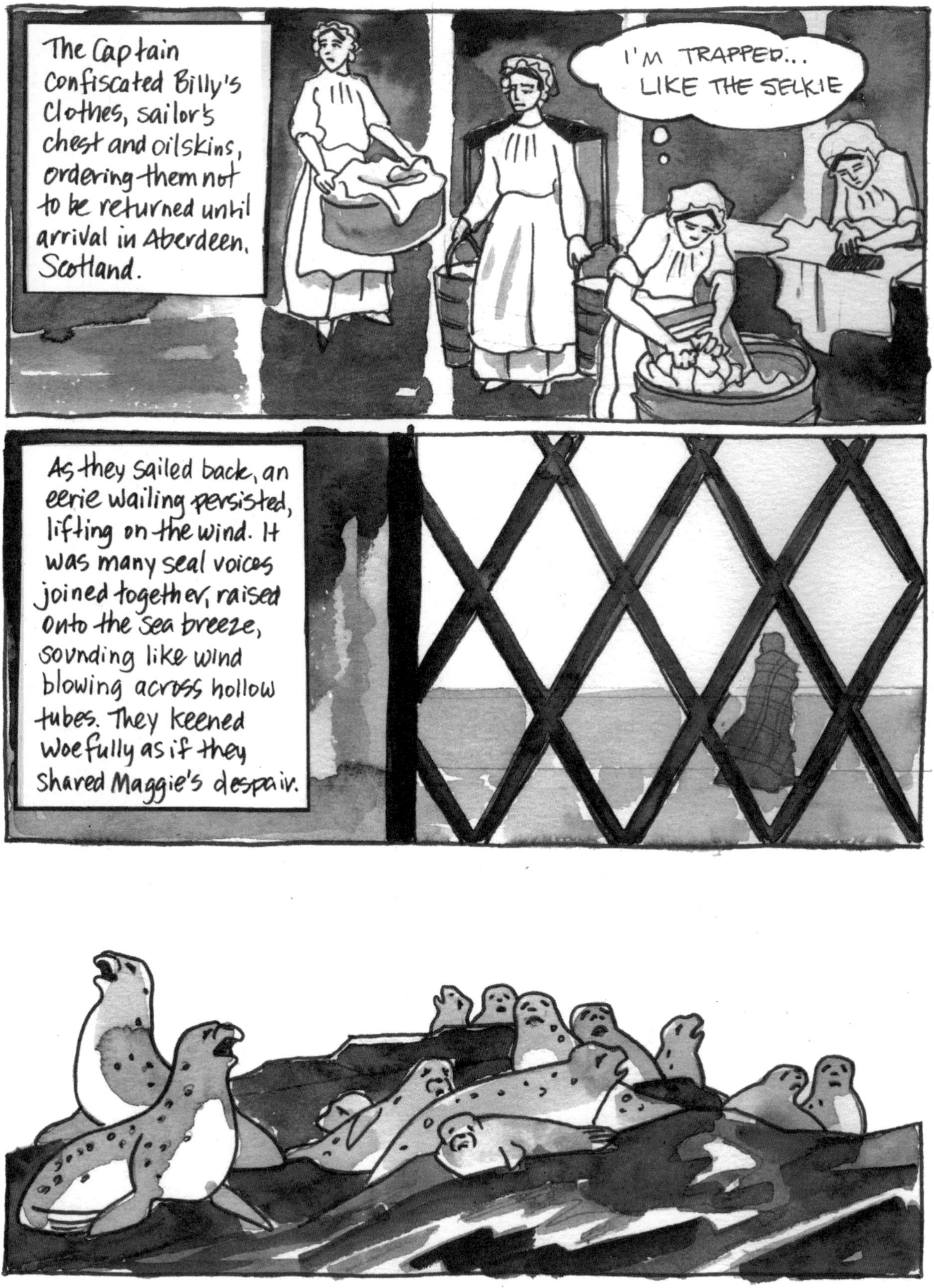
The Captain confiscated Billy's clothes, sailor's chest and oilskins, ordering them not to be returned until arrival in Aberdeen. Scotland.
I'M TRAPPED... LIKE THE SELKIE
As they sailed back, an eerie wailing persisted, lifting on the wind. It was many seal voices joined together, raised onto the sea breeze, sounding like wind blowing across hollow tubes. They keened woefully as if they shared Maggie's despair.

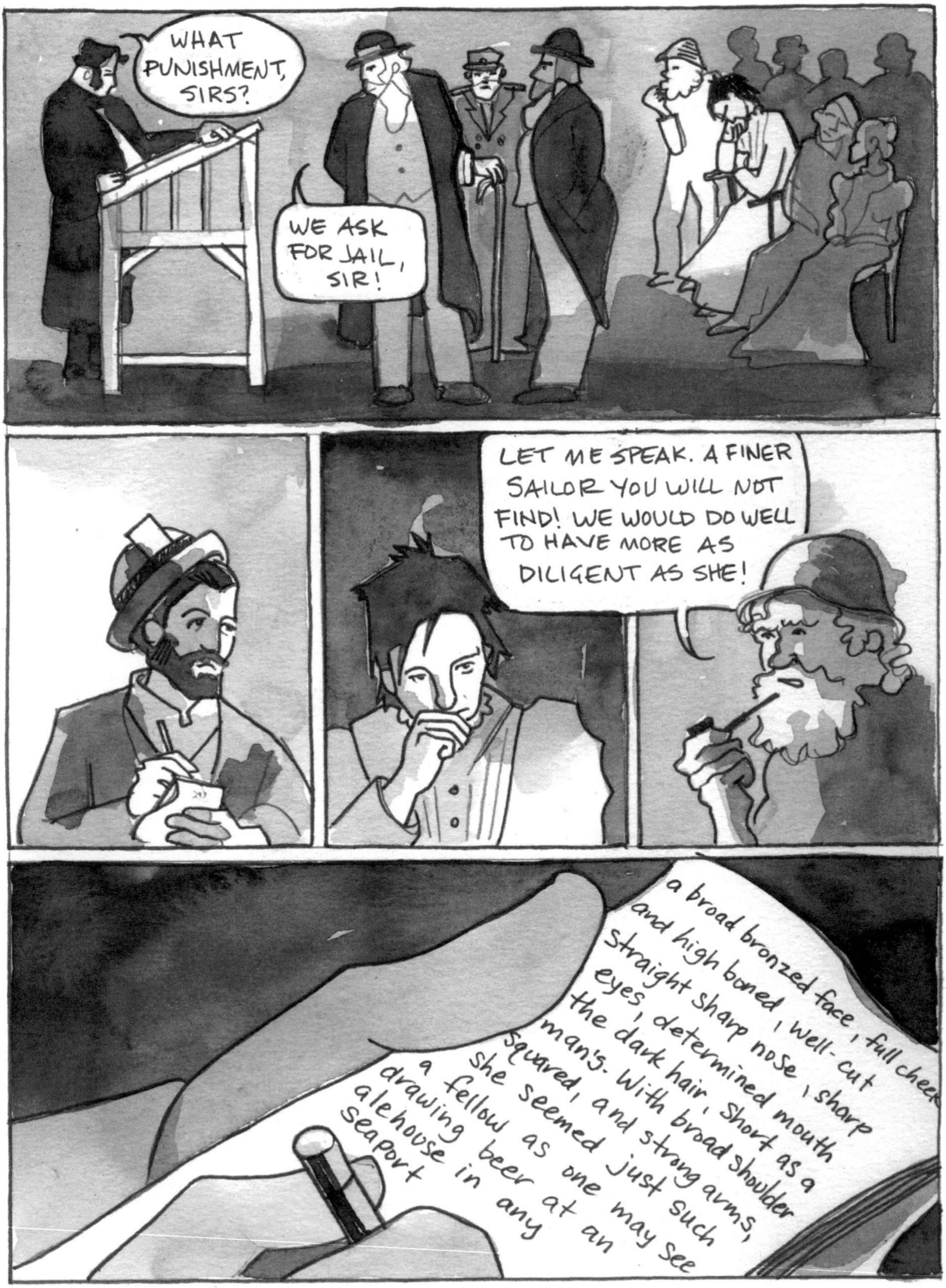
WHAT PUNISHMENT, SIRS?
WE ASK FOR JAIL, SIR!
LET ME SPEAK. A FINER SAILOR YOU WILL NOT FIND! WE WOULD DO WELL TO HAVE MORE AS DILIGENT AS SHE!
a broad bronzed face, full cheek and high boned, well-cut straight sharp nose, sharp eyes, determined mouth the dark hair, short as a man's. With broad shoulder squared, and strong arms, she seemed just such a fellow as one may see drawing beer at an alehouse in any seaport

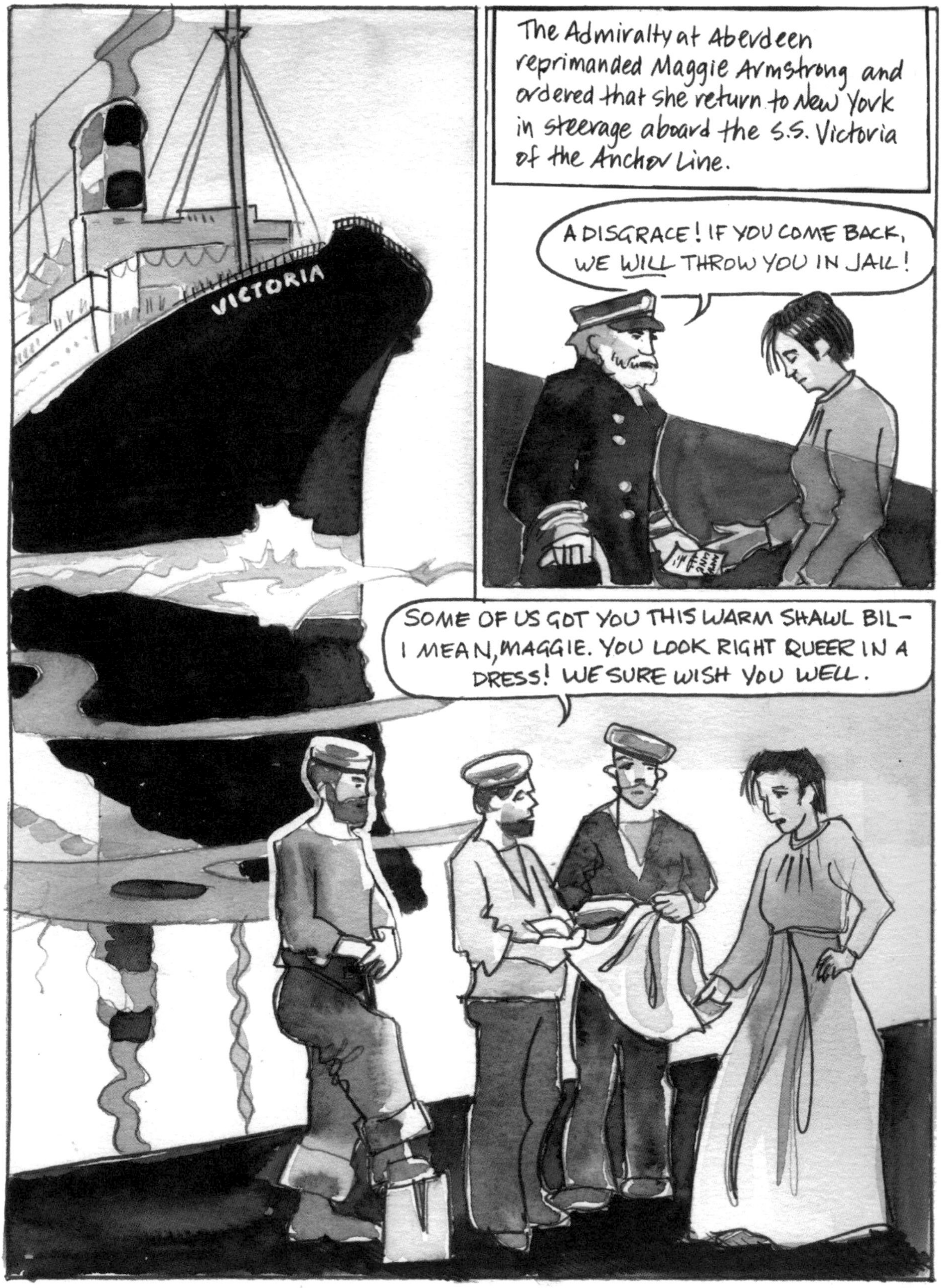
VICTORIA
The Admiralty at Aberdeen reprimanded Maggie Armstrong and ordered that she return to New York in steerage aboard the S.S. Victoria of the Anchor Line.
A DISGRACE! IF YOU COME BACK, WE WILL THROW YOU IN JAIL!
SOME OF US GOT YOU THIS WARM SHAWL BIL- I MEAN, MAGGIE. YOU LOOK RIGHT QUEER IN A DRESS! WE SURE WISH YOU WELL.

ABERDEEN JOURNAL

22 January 1873

A FEMALE SAILOR — The appearance of such a phenomenon as this is too rare an occurrence here to pass unnoticed. The "lady sailor," as she has been respectfully styled by the seafaring community to some days past, arrived here on Friday evening, on board the ship Eskdale, of Whitby, from Malaga, with Esparto grass. Her life for some time past has been rather of a romantic character. Her parents, who are Dutch origin, live in New Jersey, U.S., and her mother having died, her father married again. Finding life under the new government hard to bear, she conceived the bold idea of shifting for herself "like a man," and with a suit of her father's clothes, and a small sum of money, she found her way to New York. Assuming the name of William Armstrong. Margaret, who is now only nineteen, got shipped as engineer's steward on board the Hutton, a steamer belonging to Newcastle, at 15s per week. She sailed on the 1st July, 1872, for London, where the whole of the crew were discharged, and she with the rest. Still disguising her sex, she walked to Shields, where she shipped on board the Eskdale of Whitby, as an apprentice for three years. The Eskdale sailed for Genoa, with a cargo of coals, and it was not till the arrival of the ship at her destination that her real sex was discovered. The captain's wife was the first to hint a suspicion, which received confirmation every day from a close observation of her habits. She was always the last to turn in and first to turn out, and invariably slept with her clothes on. The truth came out at Genoa, and before the English Consul she signed herself as stewardess. The Eskdale left Genoa for Malaga, shipped a cargo of grass and sailed for this port where she arrived, as stated, on Friday last. Up till the time that the discovery was made, Margaret has passed as William for three months and five days. Her character as a seaman was all that could be desired, and she states that after the first time she went aloft which caused her serious anxiety, she thought nothing about it, and at scrubbing the decks and scraping the masts she proved herself remarkably useful. Margaret was a strong masculine appearance, a tawny Dutch countenance, and in stature she towers above several of the crew. She was kindly treated by all on board, but she has no great liking after all for the seafaring life, and will be glad to get safely back to her home. Having received an advance at the commencement of the voyage, she had no wages to receive, but on getting her discharge at the Shipping office, Mr. Inglis, and some gentlemen connected with shipping, subscribed a few pounds in her behalf, and had her decently attired and sent to Glasgow, where the American Consul will doubtless get her a berth to New York.

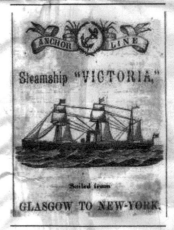

ANCHOR LINE

Steamship "VICTORIA,"

Sailed from

GLASGOW TO NEW-YORK.

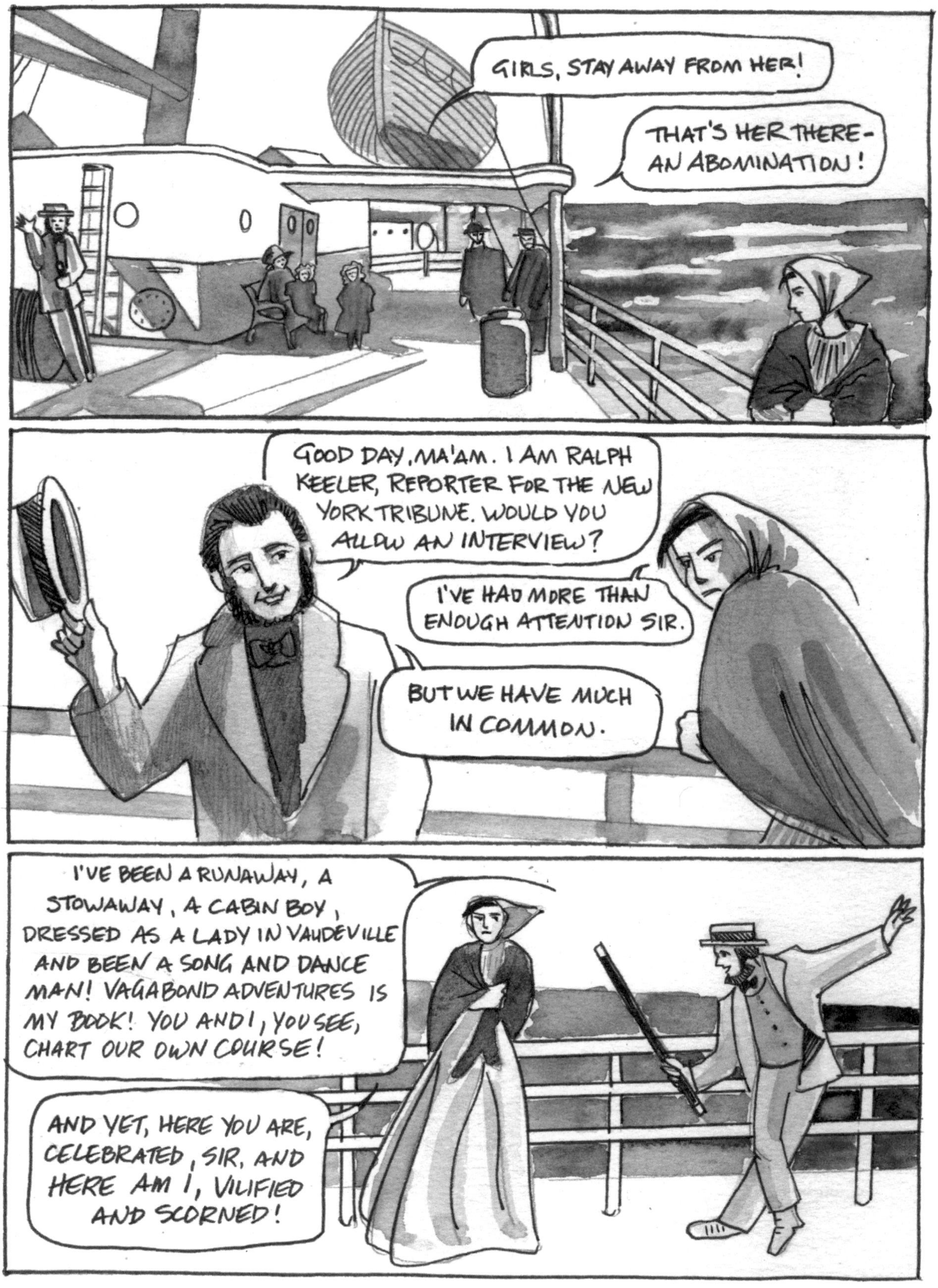
GIRLS, STAY AWAY FROM HER!
THAT'S HER THERE - AN ABOMINATION!
GOOD DAY, MA'AM. I AM RALPH KEELER, REPORTER FOR THE NEW YORK TRIBUNE. WOULD YOU ALLOW AN INTERVIEW?
I'VE HAD MORE THAN ENOUGH ATTENTION SIR.
BUT WE HAVE MUCH IN COMMON.
I'VE BEEN A RUNAWAY, A STOWAWAY, A CABIN BOY, DRESSED AS A LADY IN VAUDEVILLE AND BEEN A SONG AND DANCE MAN! VAGABOND ADVENTURES IS MY BOOK! YOU AND I, YOU SEE, CHART OUR OWN COURSE!
AND YET, HERE YOU ARE, CELEBRATED, SIR, AND HERE AM I, VILIFIED AND SCORNED!

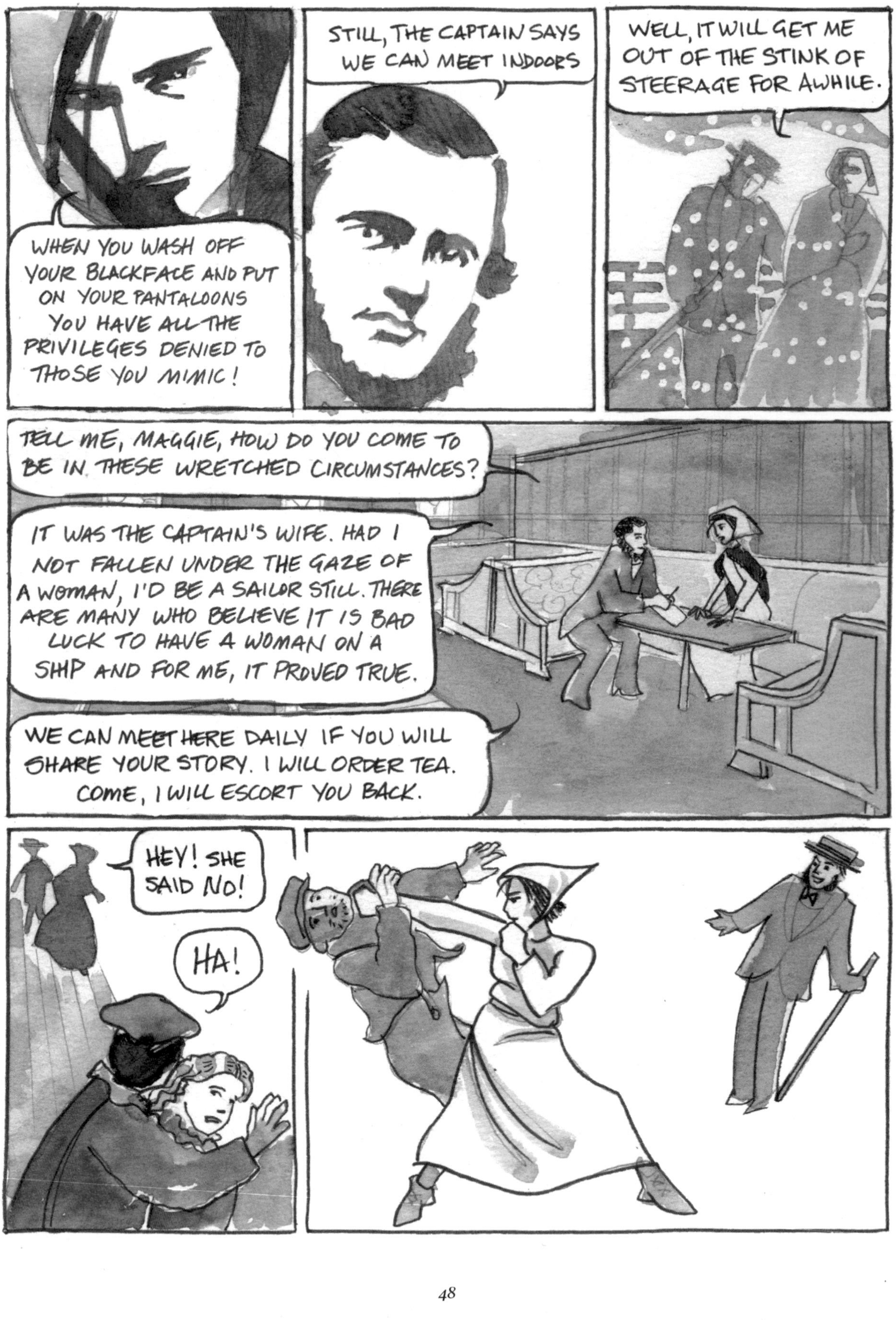

WHEN YOU WASH OFF YOUR BLACKFACE AND PUT ON YOUR PANTALOONS YOU HAVE ALL THE PRIVILEGES DENIED TO THOSE YOU MIMIC!
STILL, THE CAPTAIN SAYS WE CAN MEET INDOORS
WELL, IT WILL GET ME OUT OF THE STINK OF STEERAGE FOR AWHILE.
TELL ME, MAGGIE, HOW DO YOU COME TO BE IN THESE WRETCHED CIRCUMSTANCES?
IT WAS THE CAPTAIN'S WIFE. HAD I NOT FALLEN UNDER THE GAZE OF A WOMAN, I'D BE A SAILOR STILL. THERE ARE MANY WHO BELIEVE IT IS BAD LUCK TO HAVE A WOMAN ON A SHIP AND FOR ME, IT PROVED TRUE.
WE CAN MEET HERE DAILY IF YOU WILL SHARE YOUR STORY. I WILL ORDER TEA. COME, I WILL ESCORT YOU BACK.
HEY! SHE SAID NO!
HA!

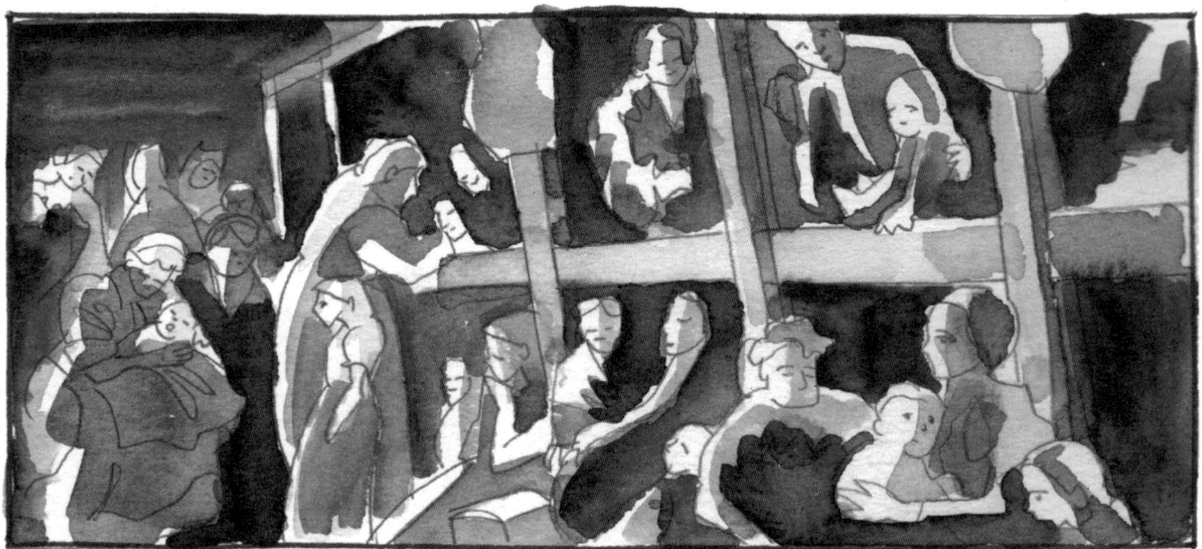

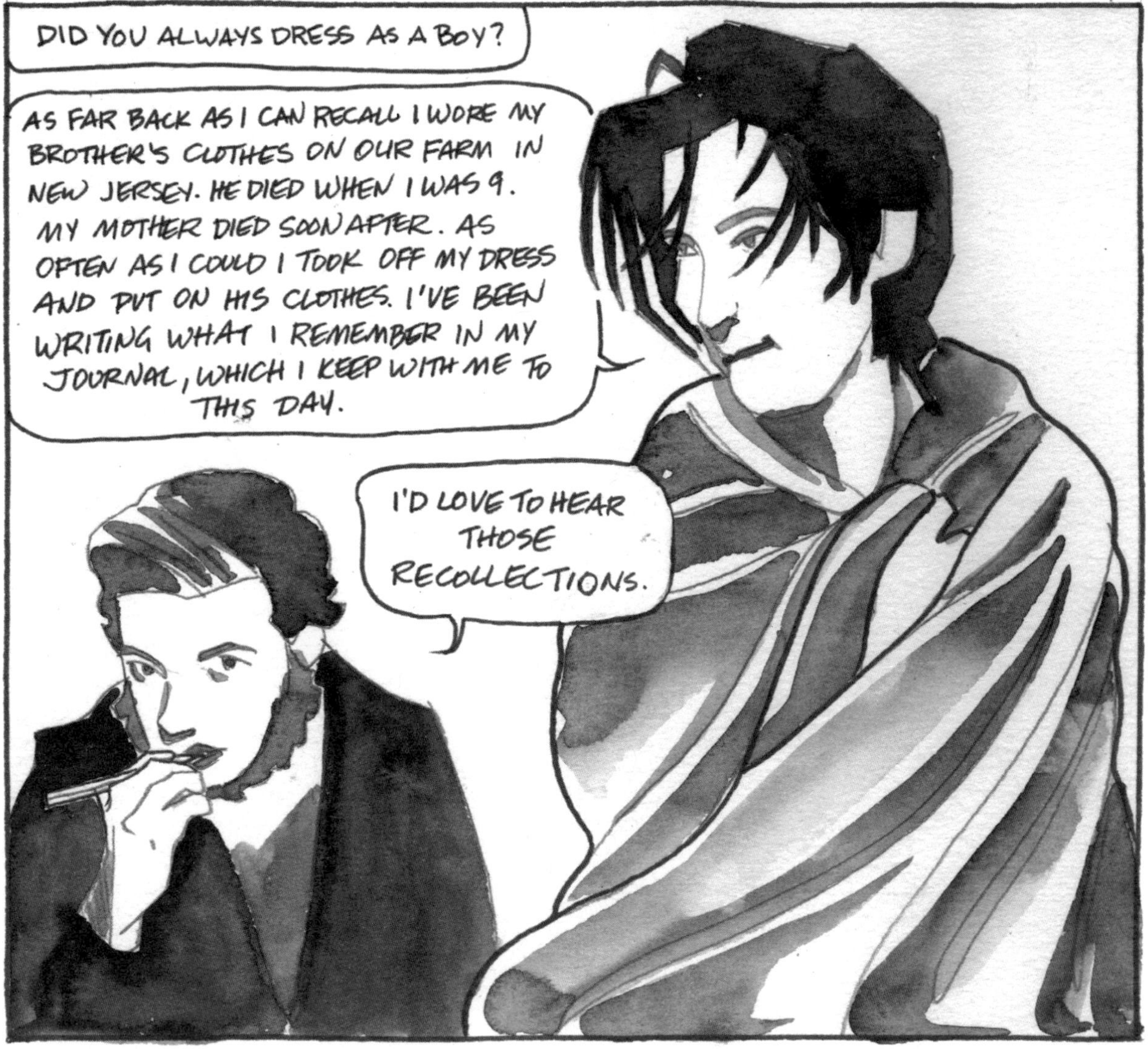
DID YOU ALWAYS DRESS AS A BOY?
AS FAR BACK AS I CAN RECALL I WORE MY BROTHER'S CLOTHES ON OUR FARM IN NEW JERSEY. HE DIED WHEN I WAS 9. MY MOTHER DIED SOON AFTER. AS OFTEN AS I COULD I TOOK OFF MY DRESS AND PUT ON HIS CLOTHES. I'VE BEEN WRITING WHAT I REMEMBER IN MY JOURNAL, WHICH I KEEP WITH ME TO THIS DAY.
I'D LOVE TO HEAR THOSE RECOLLECTIONS.

"My name" she says, "is Mago
put on my pantaloons. I was
father is a farmer five mil
times that I could do m
wild passionate nature. I wa
thought they ought not to
wished I was a man. My
little sister and me. Fath
to do his work. When I
a notion to get a wi
came to our hou
but I soon taught h
to hire ... out
after me and took
a cat and dog life
endure that long so
was up stairs. As
engaged clearing u
to her that if I
have a job to find
was silence betwe
saying anything
to try it. At 2
mean, I went i
clothes. I took
I could, and t
out of one of
no use going
station and took
about the city a
street I think. I
what to do for
one of those r
a freight steam
back to New Yo
as I was cur
steward. I nev
was so well b
I always use
time at home
engineers were
informed me
York but on
discharged at
engineer presence
good clean lad, had
I was able to live
to all over the great
soon as I learned that
I made up my mind that I

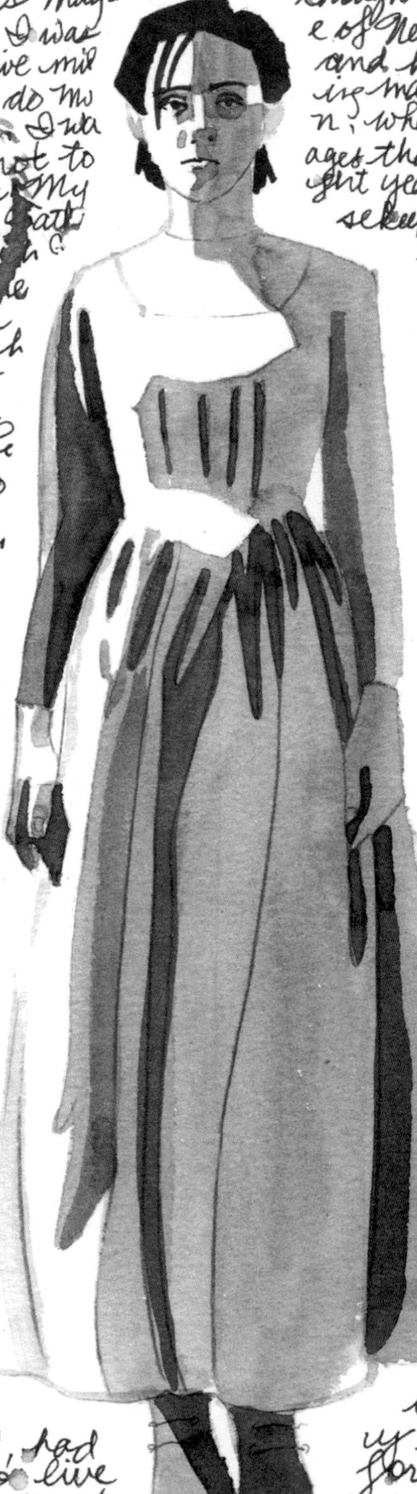

though I call myself Billy when I
e of New Jersey, America. My
and he has told me hundreds
ing man. I was always of a
n; when I was at home. I
ages than women, and I often
girl years ago, and left another
sekeeper until I was able
last April when he took
got in New York. She
I me and everything.
the house and went
o. My father came
light days leading
I thought I could not
into my head. I
schoolmate. I was
lonely, and I said
his clothes he would
and he would. There
s, and without
secretly determined
e next morning. I
in my father's
air as short as I
ger and took $25
I knew it was
I went to the
rk. I wandered
nall hotel on Warren
make up my mind
York before when
me to ship on
to London and
nd to suit me
me as engineer's
fact, I never
been at sea.
in the summer.
1. All the
way. But they
back to New
a. So I was
on the head
ungs for being a
y wages, 15 shillings
for 3 weeks. I went
v no end of things as
me was going to China
had to get back to America.

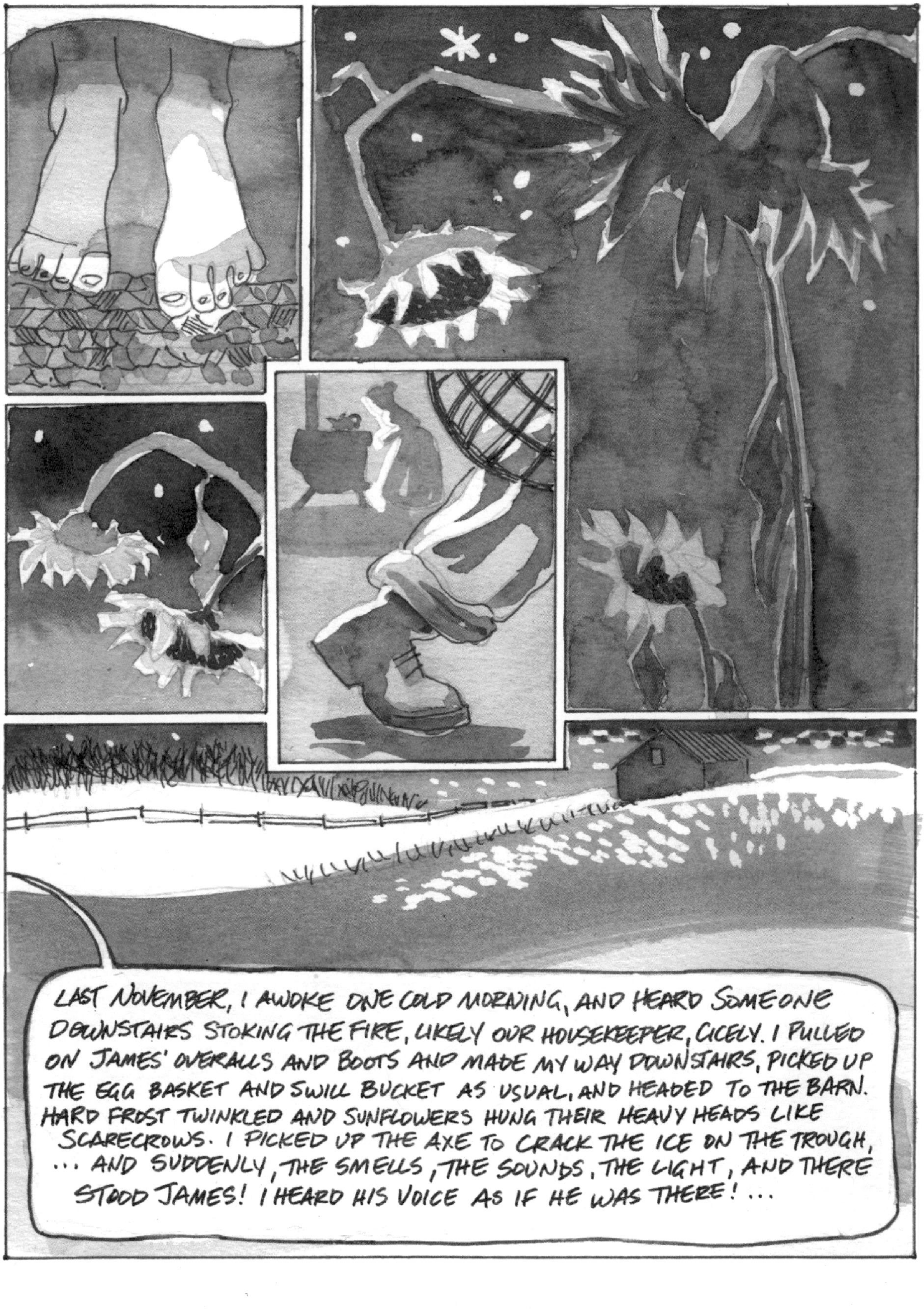
LAST NOVEMBER, I AWOKE ONE COLD MORNING, AND HEARD SOMEONE DOWNSTAIRS STOKING THE FIRE, LIKELY OUR HOUSEKEEPER, CICELY. I PULLED ON JAMES' OVERALLS AND BOOTS AND MADE MY WAY DOWNSTAIRS, PICKED UP THE EGG BASKET AND SWILL BUCKET AS USUAL, AND HEADED TO THE BARN. HARD FROST TWINKLED AND SUNFLOWERS HUNG THEIR HEAVY HEADS LIKE SCARECROWS. I PICKED UP THE AXE TO CRACK THE ICE ON THE TROUGH, ... AND SUDDENLY, THE SMELLS, THE SOUNDS, THE LIGHT, AND THERE STOOD JAMES! I HEARD HIS VOICE AS IF HE WAS THERE! ...

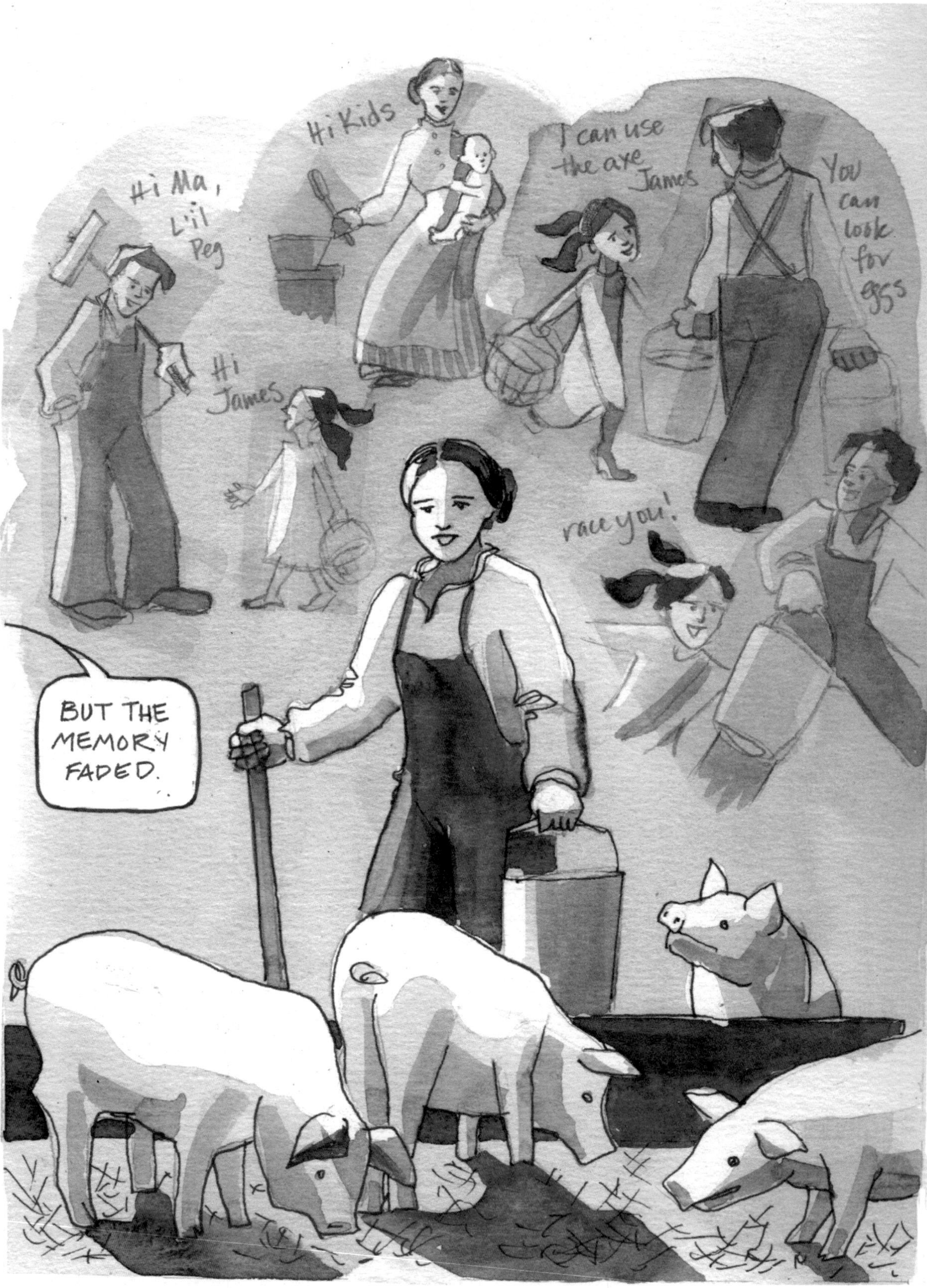
Hi Ma, L'il Peg
Hi Kids
I can use the axe James
You can look for eggs
Hi James
race you!
BUT THE MEMORY FADED.

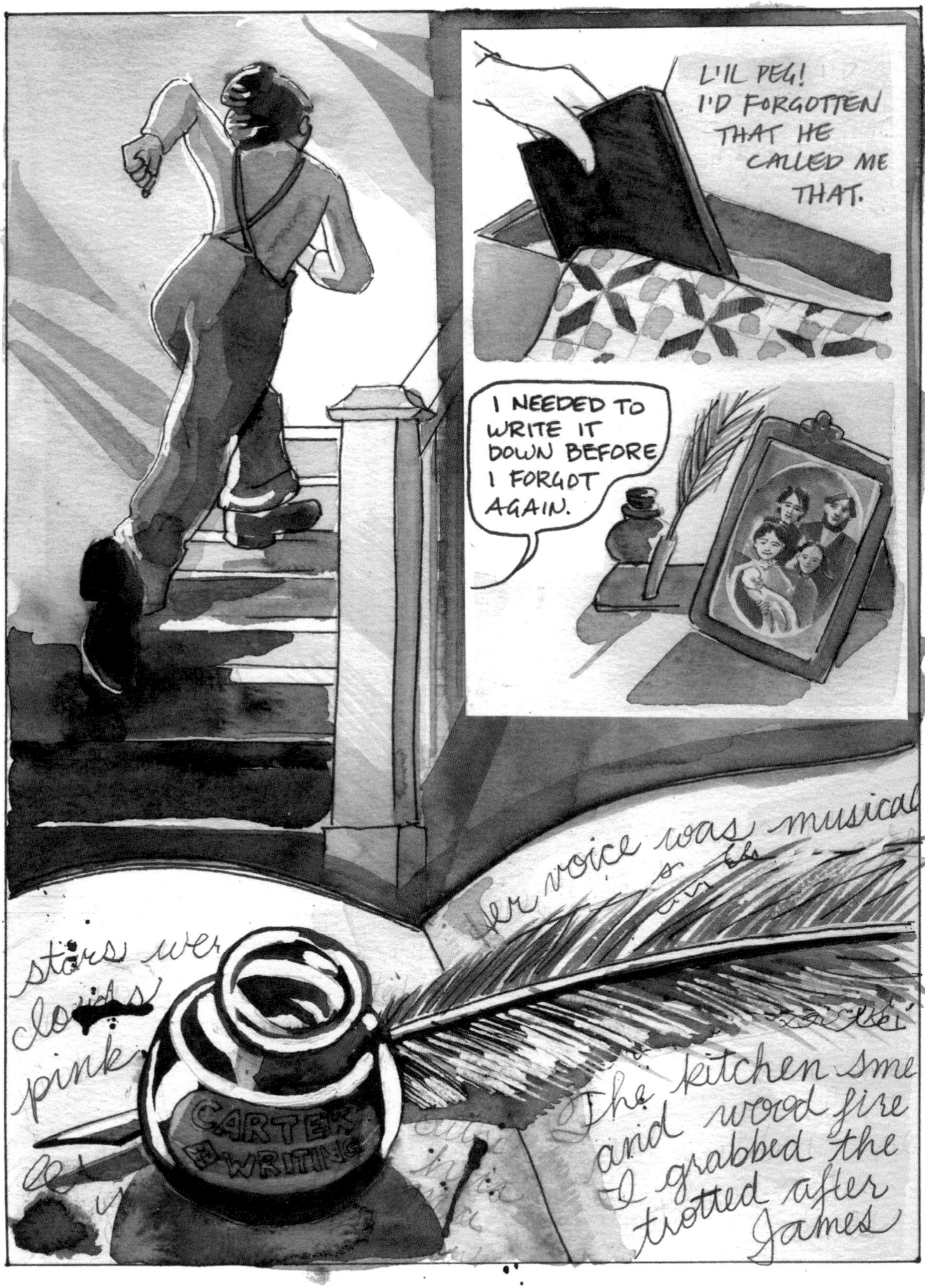
L'IL PEG! I'D FORGOTTEN THAT HE CALLED ME THAT.
I NEEDED TO WRITE IT DOWN BEFORE I FORGOT AGAIN.
Her voice was musical
stars wer
pink
The kitchen sme
and wood fire
I grabbed the
trotted after
James
CARTER'S WRITING

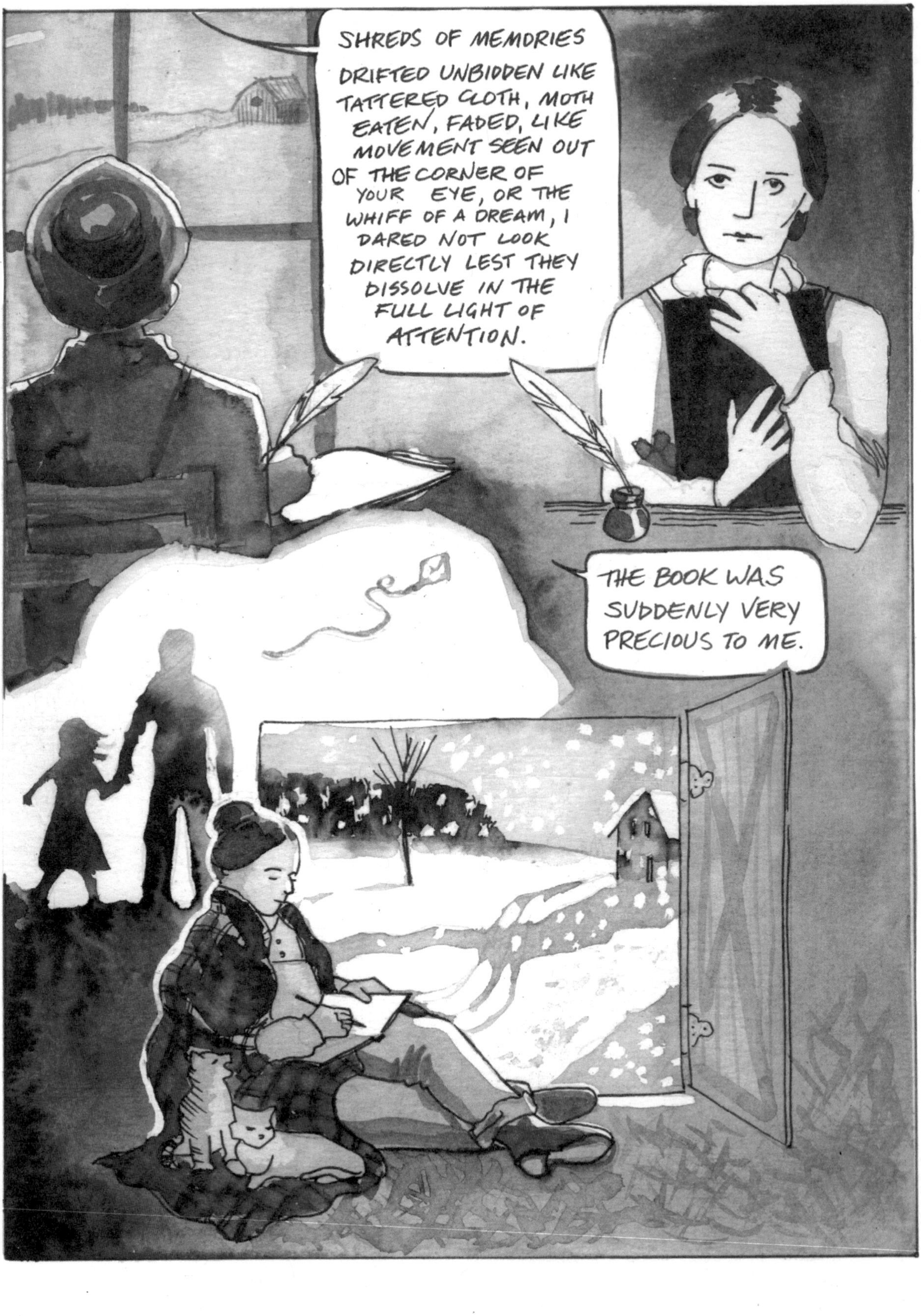
SHREDS OF MEMORIES DRIFTED UNBIDDEN LIKE TATTERED CLOTH, MOTH EATEN, FADED, LIKE MOVEMENT SEEN OUT OF THE CORNER OF YOUR EYE, OR THE WHIFF OF A DREAM, I DARED NOT LOOK DIRECTLY LEST THEY DISSOLVE IN THE FULL LIGHT OF ATTENTION.
THE BOOK WAS SUDDENLY VERY PRECIOUS TO ME.

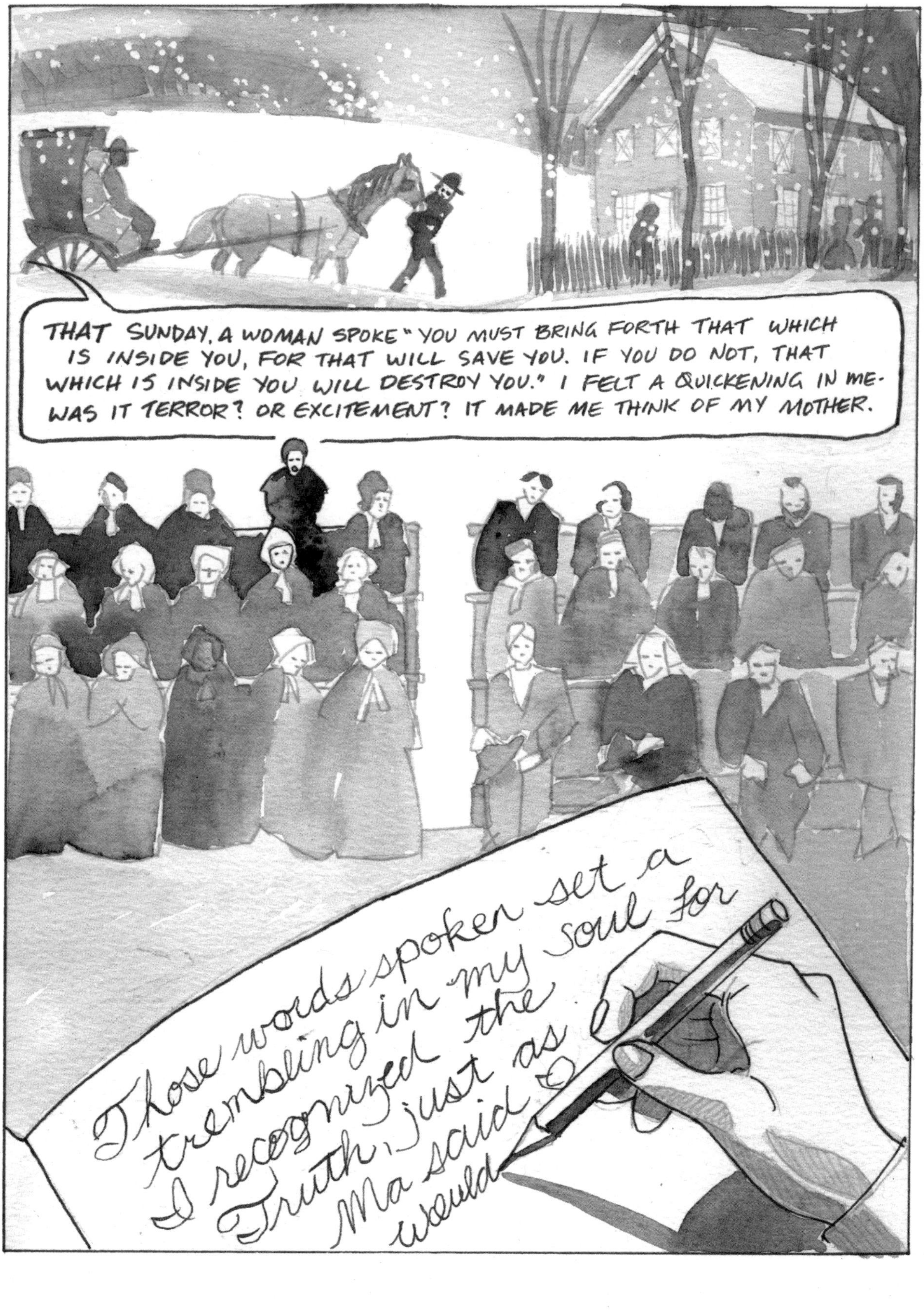
THAT SUNDAY, A WOMAN SPOKE "YOU MUST BRING FORTH THAT WHICH IS INSIDE YOU, FOR THAT WILL SAVE YOU. IF YOU DO NOT, THAT WHICH IS INSIDE YOU WILL DESTROY YOU." I FELT A QUICKENING IN ME- WAS IT TERROR? OR EXCITEMENT? IT MADE ME THINK OF MY MOTHER.
Those words spoken set a
trembling in my soul for
I recognized the
Truth, just as
Ma said
would

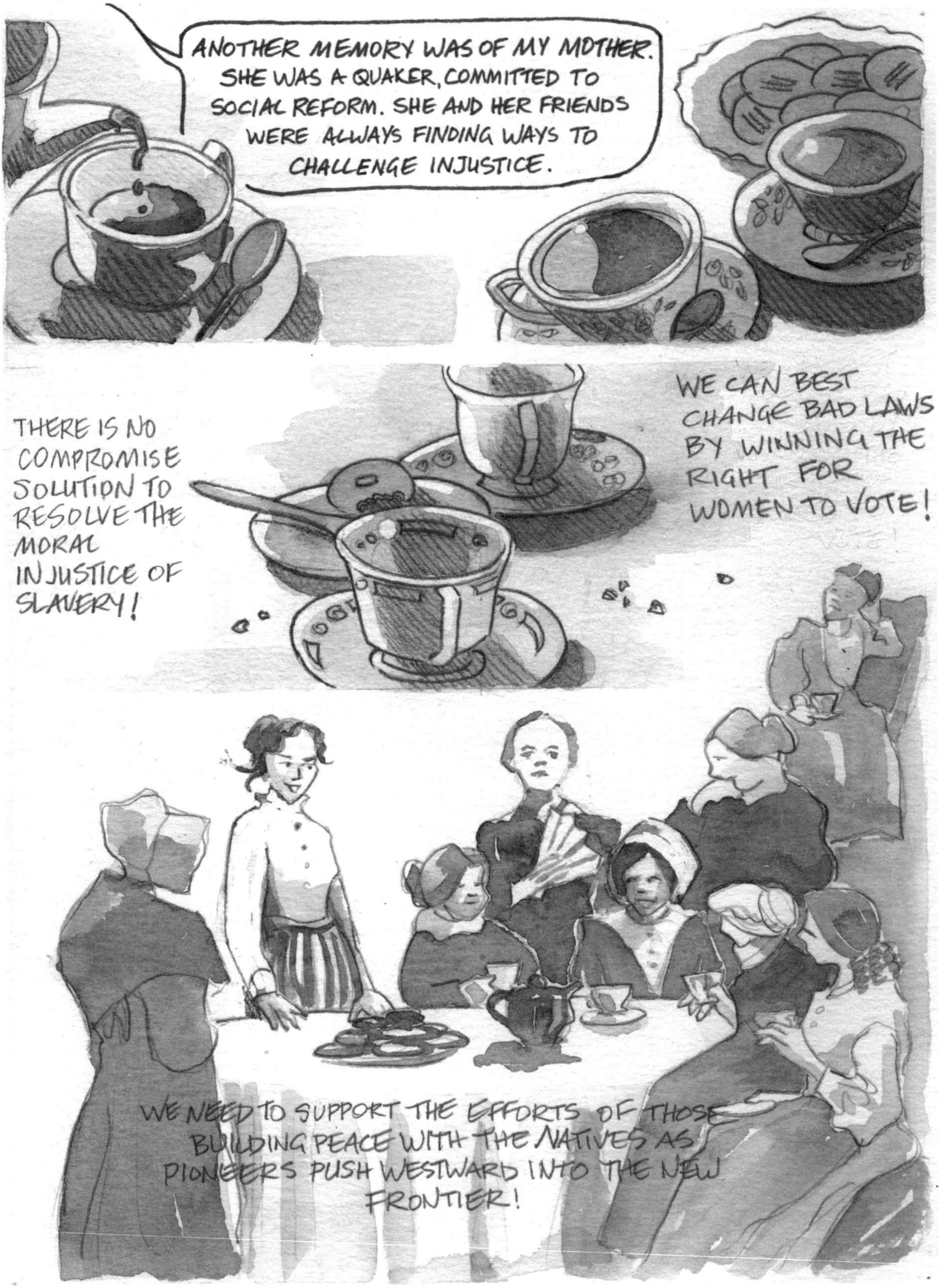
ANOTHER MEMORY WAS OF MY MOTHER. SHE WAS A QUAKER, COMMITTED TO SOCIAL REFORM. SHE AND HER FRIENDS WERE ALWAYS FINDING WAYS TO CHALLENGE INJUSTICE.
THERE IS NO COMPROMISE SOLUTION TO RESOLVE THE MORAL INJUSTICE OF SLAVERY!
WE CAN BEST CHANGE BAD LAWS BY WINNING THE RIGHT FOR WOMEN TO VOTE!
WE NEED TO SUPPORT THE EFFORTS OF THOSE BUILDING PEACE WITH THE NATIVES AS PIONEERS PUSH WESTWARD INTO THE NEW FRONTIER!

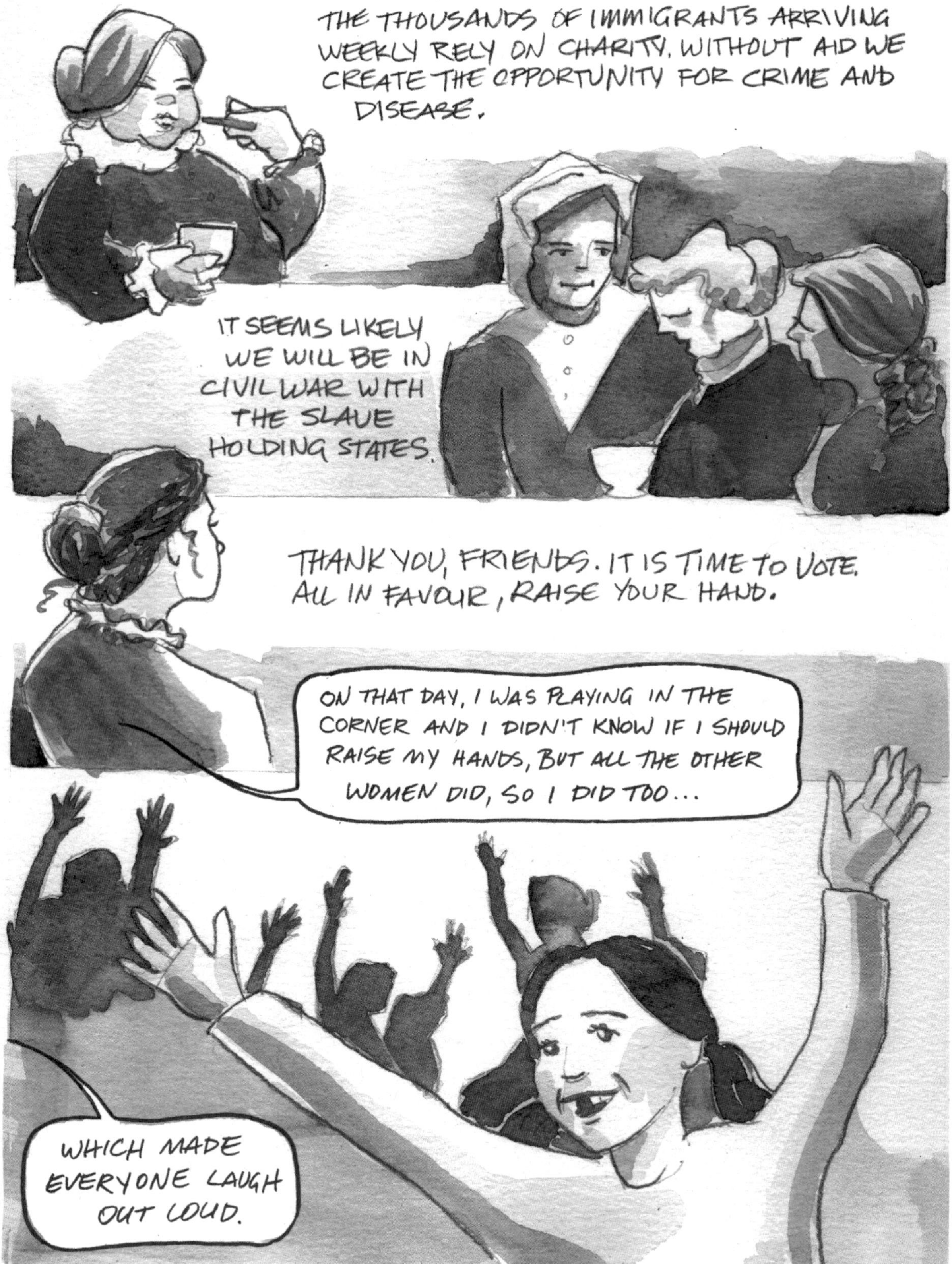
THE THOUSANDS OF IMMIGRANTS ARRIVING WEEKLY RELY ON CHARITY. WITHOUT AID WE CREATE THE OPPORTUNITY FOR CRIME AND DISEASE.
IT SEEMS LIKELY WE WILL BE IN CIVIL WAR WITH THE SLAVE HOLDING STATES.
THANK YOU, FRIENDS. IT IS TIME TO VOTE. ALL IN FAVOUR, RAISE YOUR HAND.
ON THAT DAY, I WAS PLAYING IN THE CORNER AND I DIDN'T KNOW IF I SHOULD RAISE MY HANDS, BUT ALL THE OTHER WOMEN DID, SO I DID TOO...
WHICH MADE EVERYONE LAUGH OUT LOUD.

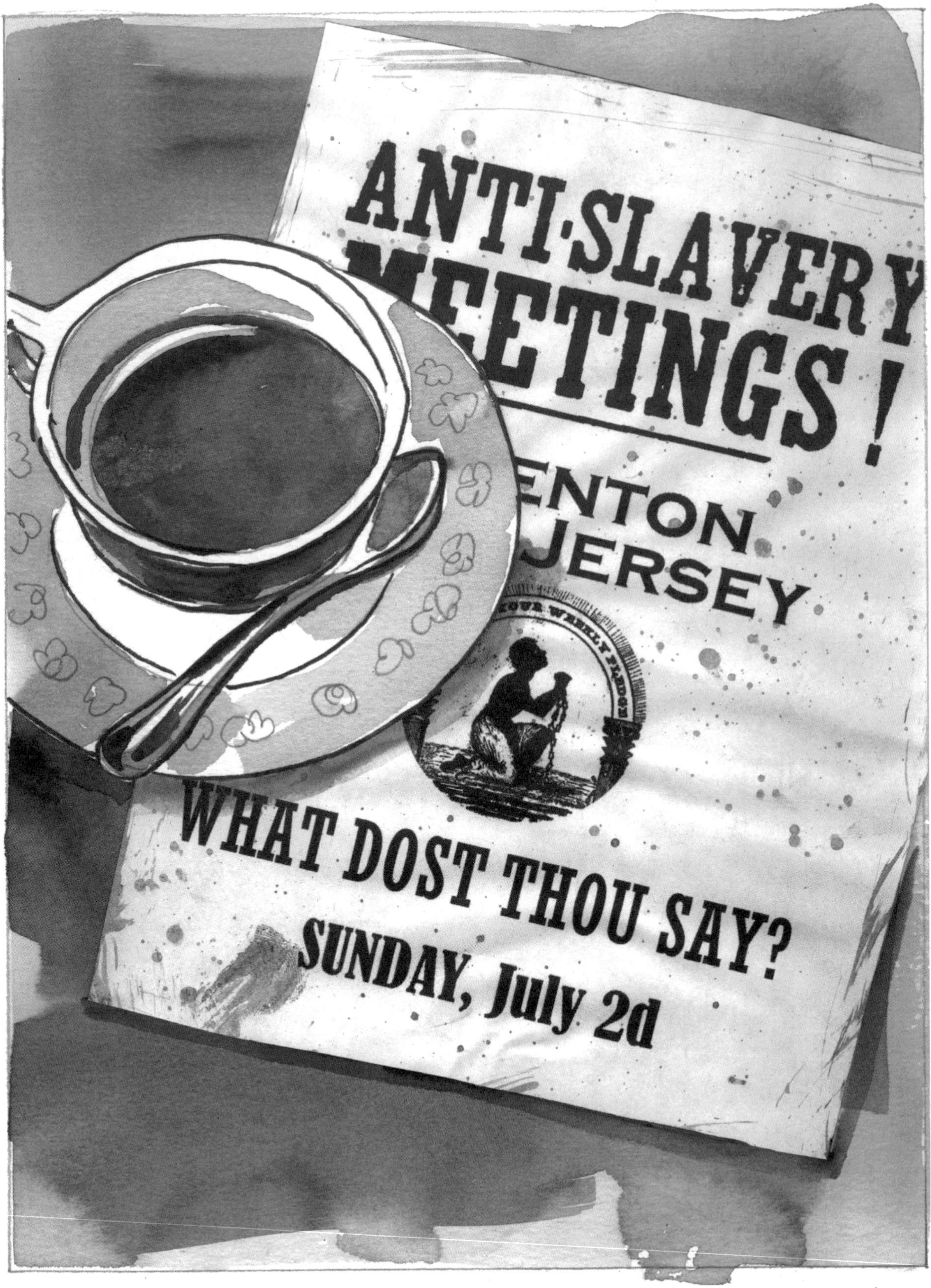
ANTI-SLAVERY
EETINGS!
ENTON
JERSEY
WHAT DOST THOU SAY?
SUNDAY, July 2d

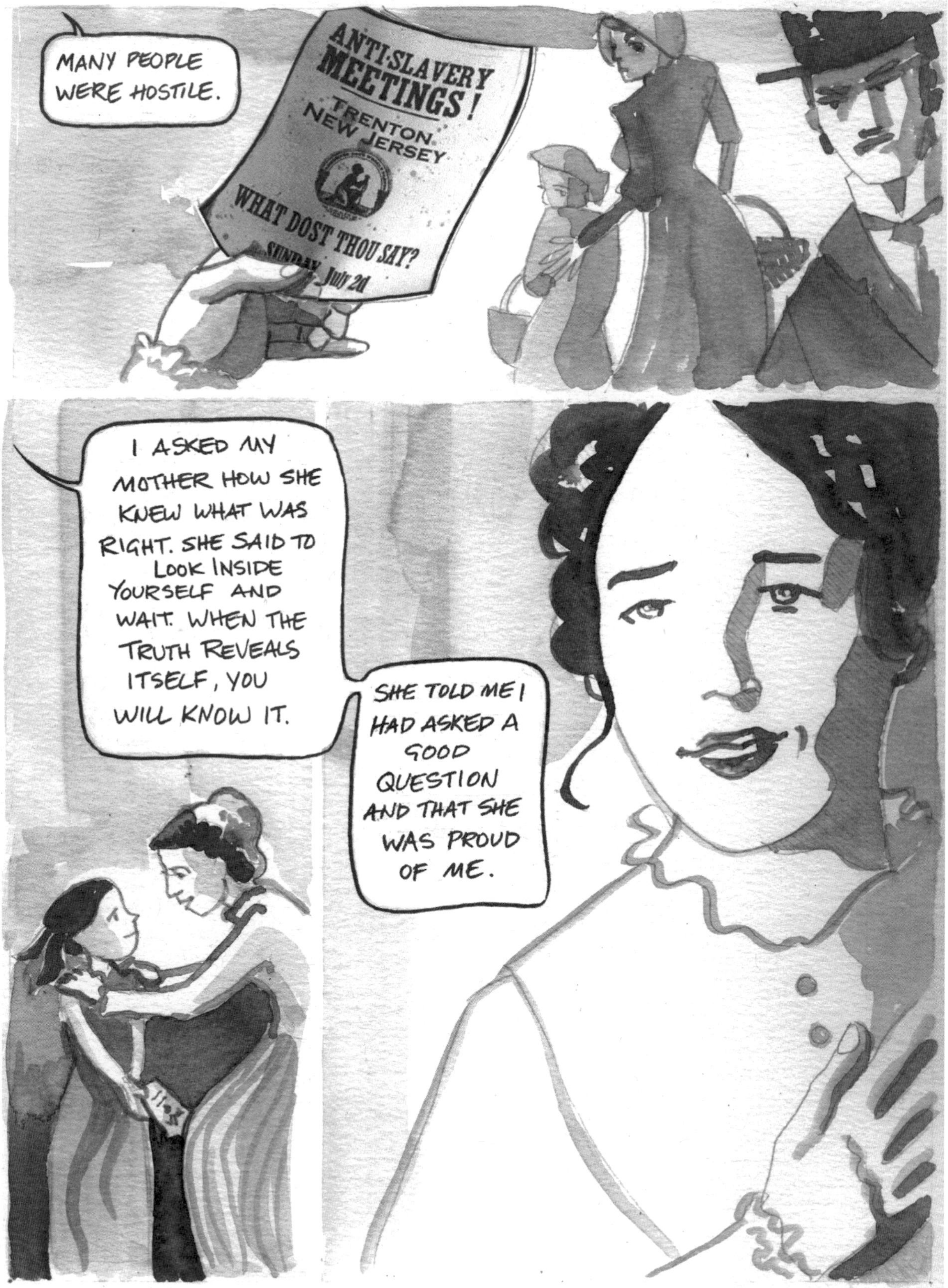
MANY PEOPLE WERE HOSTILE.
ANTI-SLAVERY MEETINGS!
TRENTON NEW JERSEY
WHAT DOST THOU SAY?
SUNDAY July 2d
I ASKED MY MOTHER HOW SHE KNEW WHAT WAS RIGHT. SHE SAID TO LOOK INSIDE YOURSELF AND WAIT. WHEN THE TRUTH REVEALS ITSELF, YOU WILL KNOW IT.
SHE TOLD ME I HAD ASKED A GOOD QUESTION AND THAT SHE WAS PROUD OF ME.

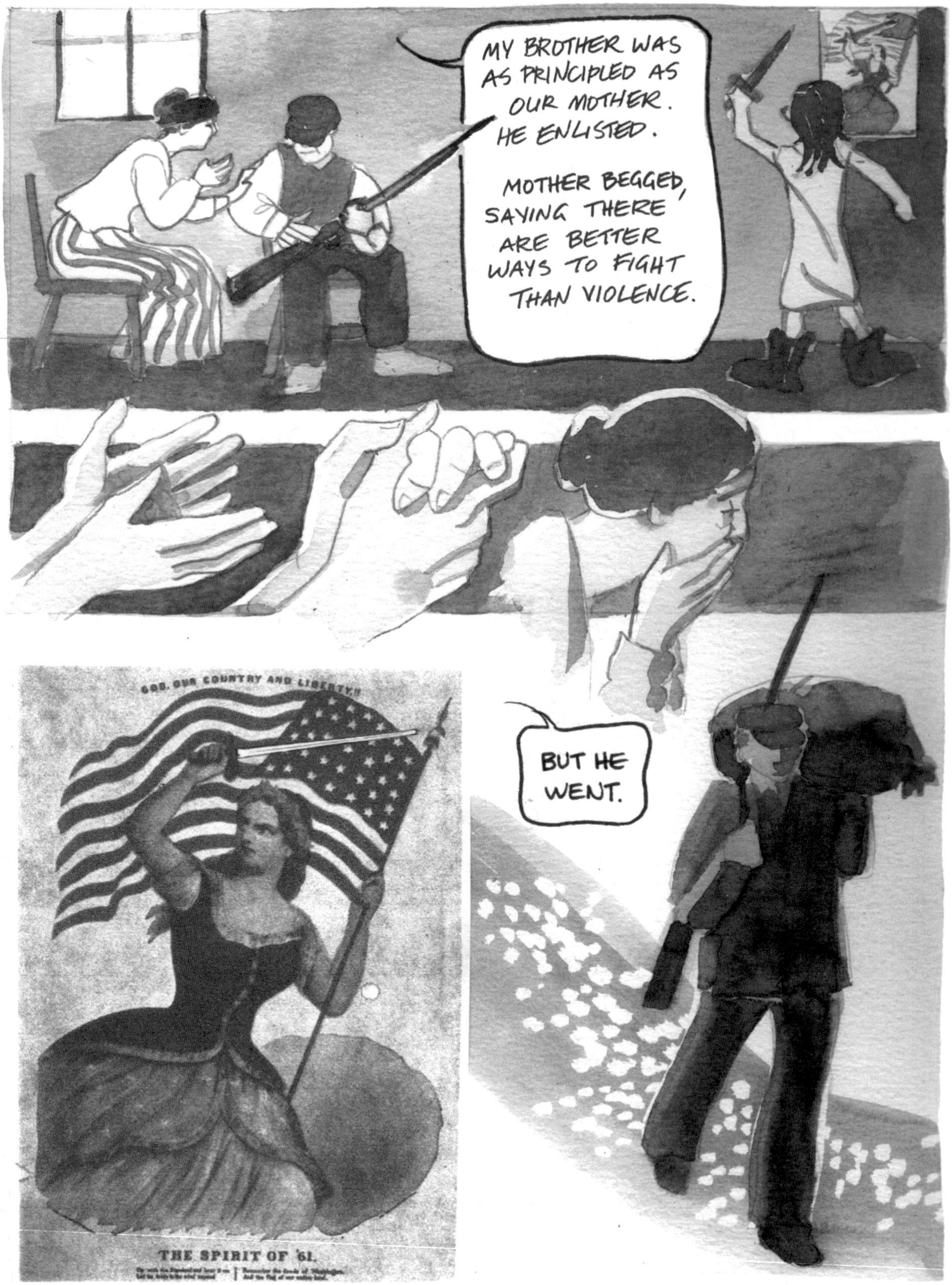
MY BROTHER WAS AS PRINCIPLED AS OUR MOTHER. HE ENLISTED.
MOTHER BEGGED, SAYING THERE ARE BETTER WAYS TO FIGHT THAN VIOLENCE.
GOD, OUR COUNTRY AND LIBERTY!!
THE SPIRIT OF '61.
BUT HE WENT.

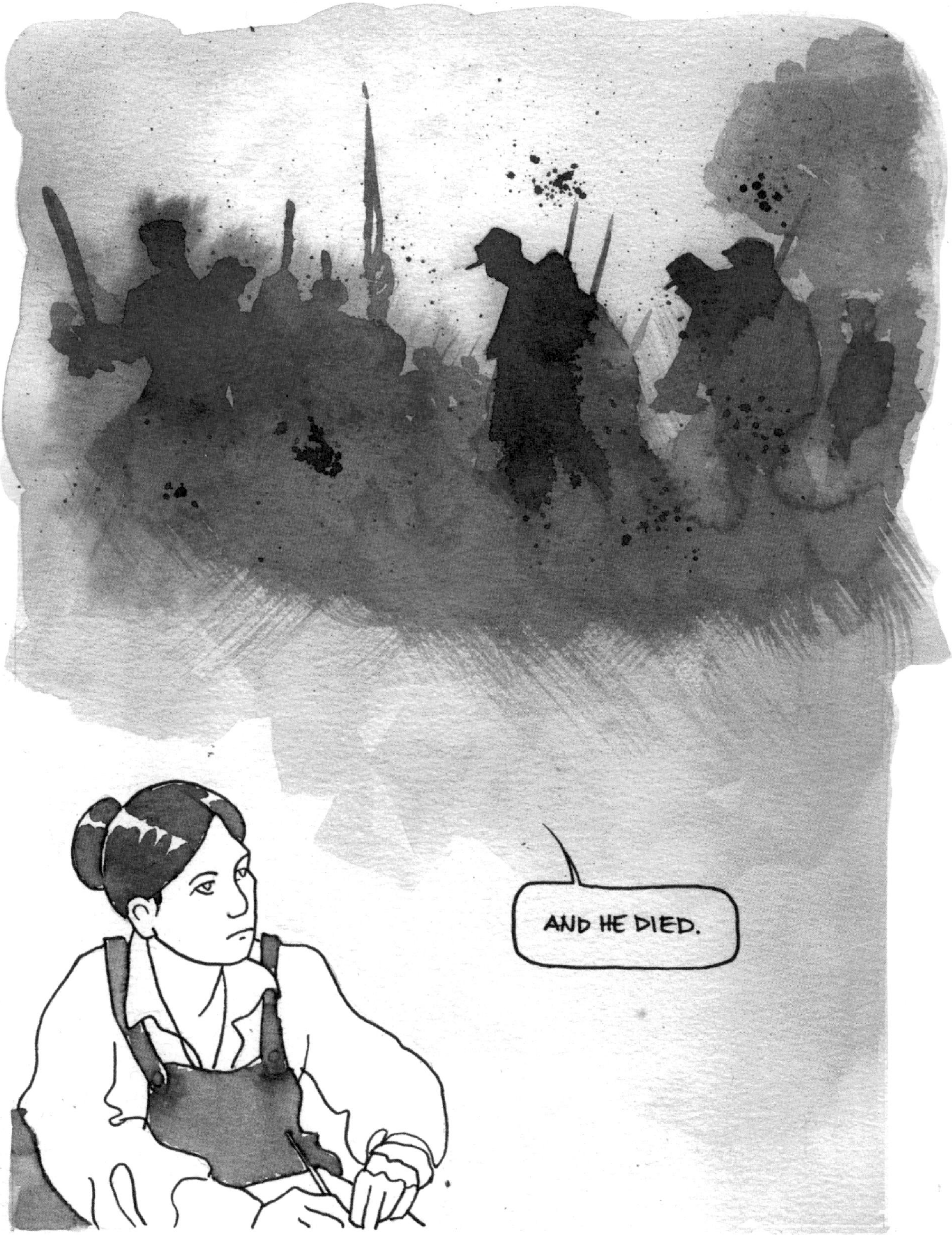
AND HE DIED.

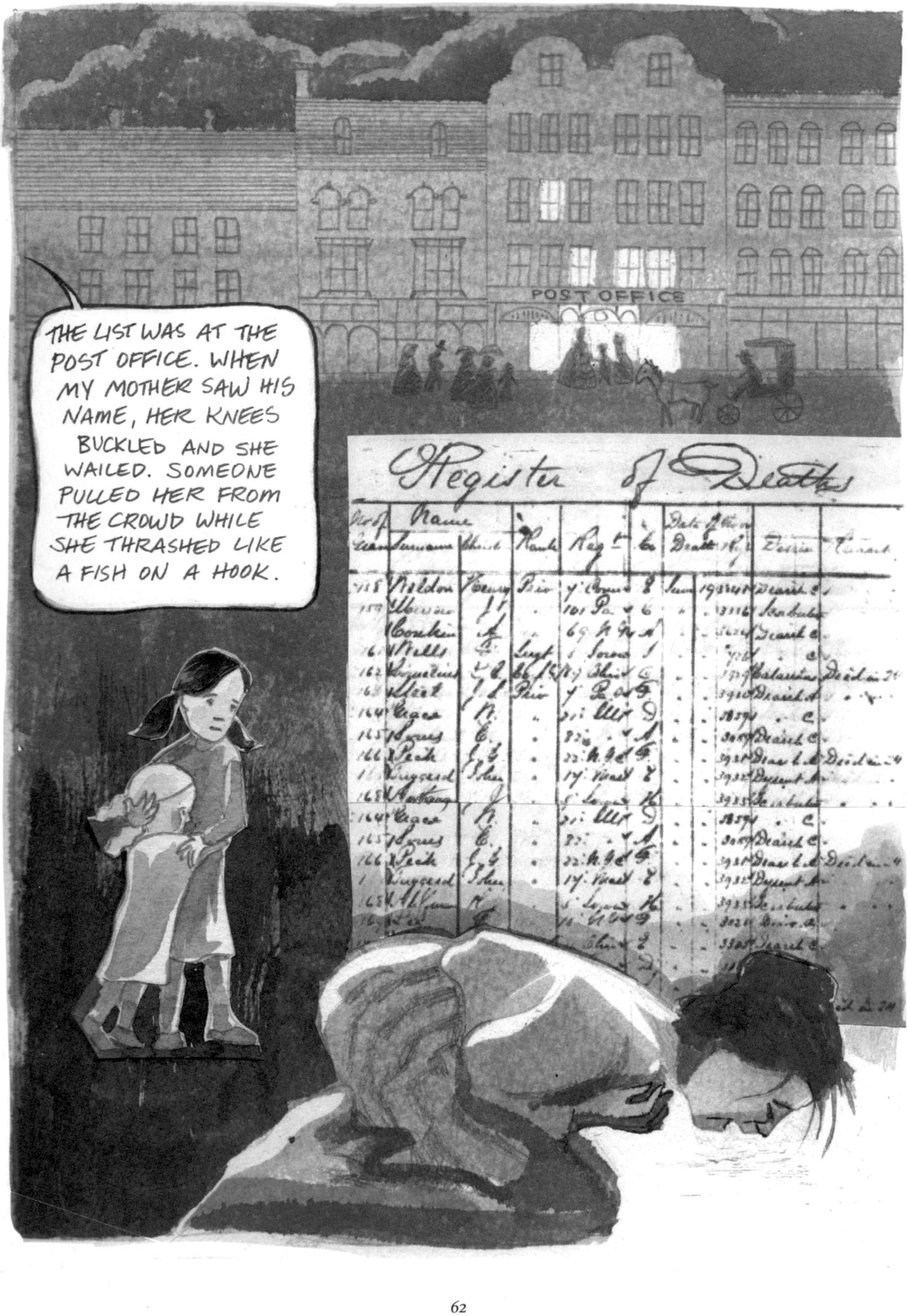
THE LIST WAS AT THE POST OFFICE. WHEN MY MOTHER SAW HIS NAME, HER KNEES BUCKLED AND SHE WAILED. SOMEONE PULLED HER FROM THE CROWD WHILE SHE THRASHED LIKE A FISH ON A HOOK.
POST OFFICE
Register of Deaths

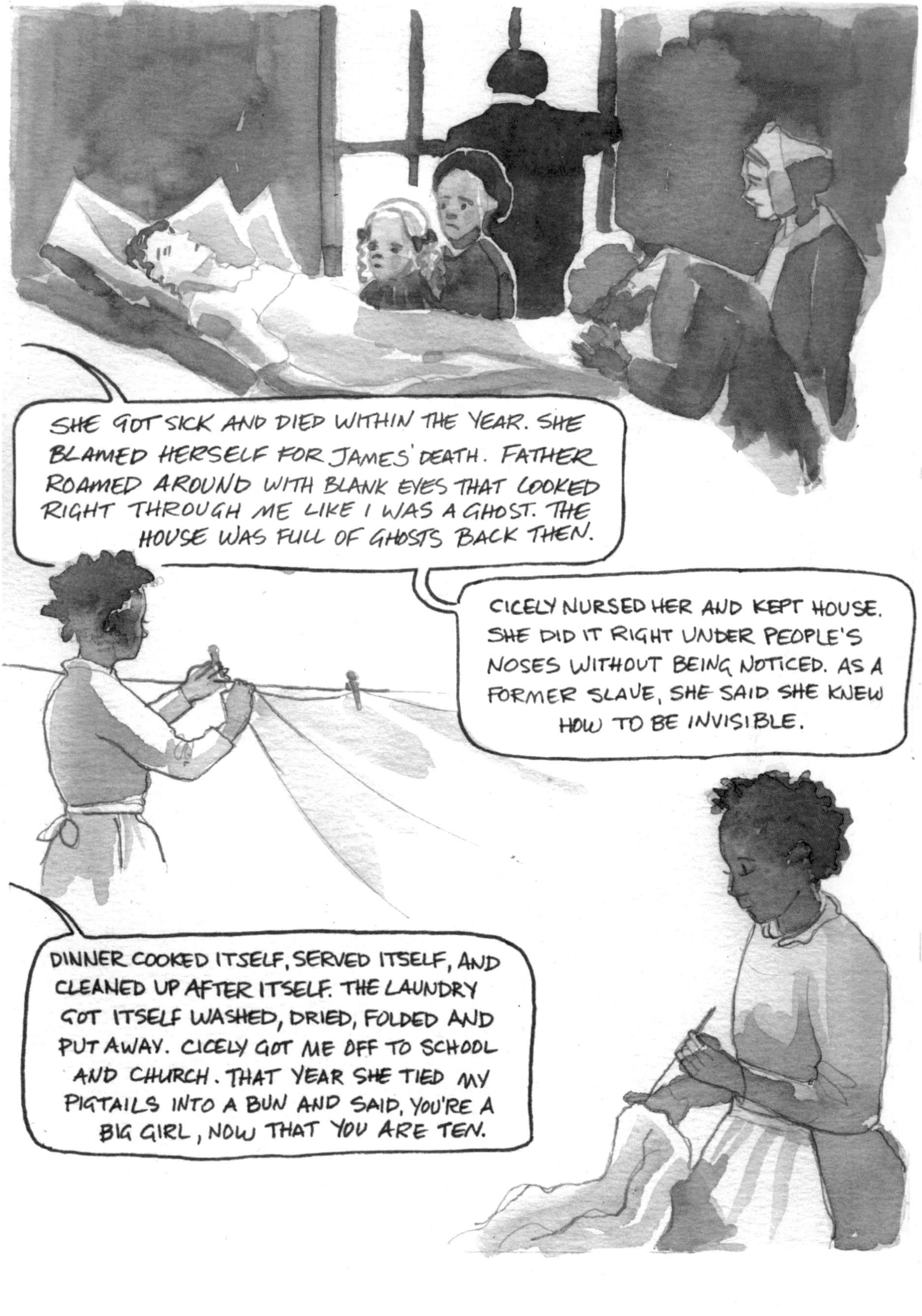
SHE GOT SICK AND DIED WITHIN THE YEAR. SHE BLAMED HERSELF FOR JAMES' DEATH. FATHER ROAMED AROUND WITH BLANK EYES THAT LOOKED RIGHT THROUGH ME LIKE I WAS A GHOST. THE HOUSE WAS FULL OF GHOSTS BACK THEN.
CICELY NURSED HER AND KEPT HOUSE. SHE DID IT RIGHT UNDER PEOPLE'S NOSES WITHOUT BEING NOTICED. AS A FORMER SLAVE, SHE SAID SHE KNEW HOW TO BE INVISIBLE.
DINNER COOKED ITSELF, SERVED ITSELF, AND CLEANED UP AFTER ITSELF. THE LAUNDRY GOT ITSELF WASHED, DRIED, FOLDED AND PUT AWAY. CICELY GOT ME OFF TO SCHOOL AND CHURCH. THAT YEAR SHE TIED MY PIGTAILS INTO A BUN AND SAID, YOU'RE A BIG GIRL, NOW THAT YOU ARE TEN.

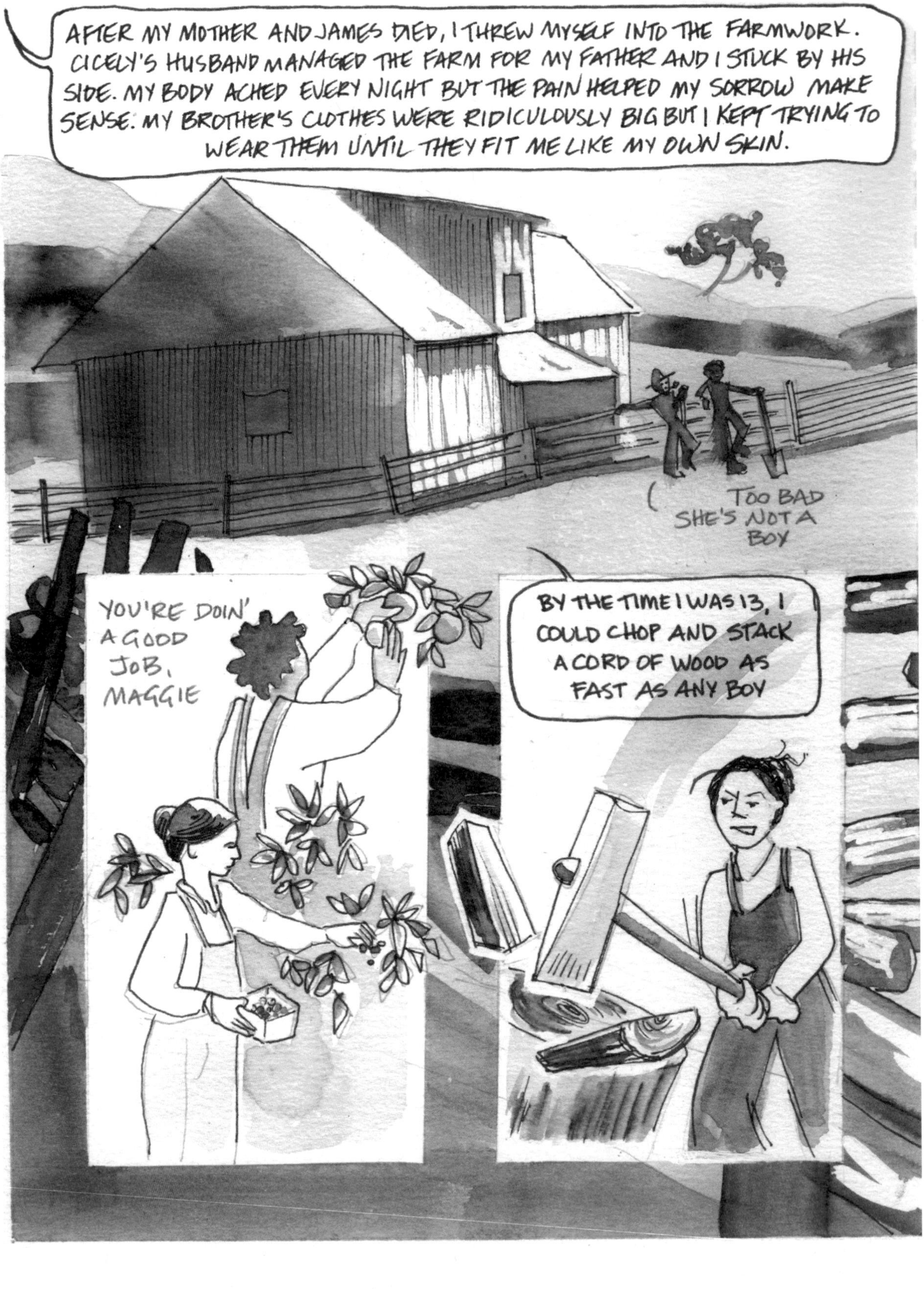
AFTER MY MOTHER AND JAMES DIED, I THREW MYSELF INTO THE FARMWORK. CICELY'S HUSBAND MANAGED THE FARM FOR MY FATHER AND I STUCK BY HIS SIDE. MY BODY ACHED EVERY NIGHT BUT THE PAIN HELPED MY SORROW MAKE SENSE. MY BROTHER'S CLOTHES WERE RIDICULOUSLY BIG BUT I KEPT TRYING TO WEAR THEM UNTIL THEY FIT ME LIKE MY OWN SKIN.
TOO BAD SHE'S NOT A BOY
YOU'RE DOIN' A GOOD JOB, MAGGIE
BY THE TIME I WAS 13, I COULD CHOP AND STACK A CORD OF WOOD AS FAST AS ANY BOY

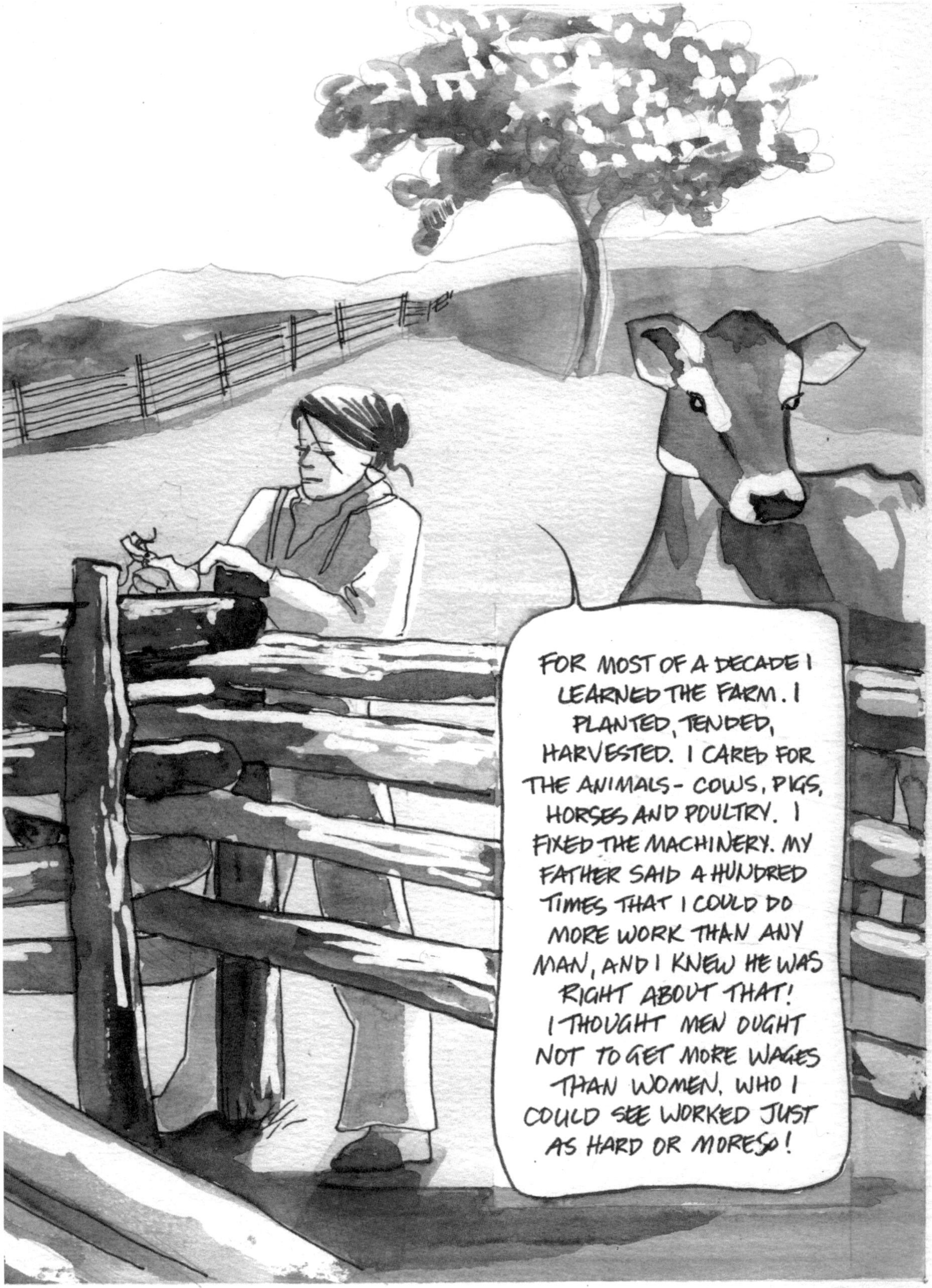
FOR MOST OF A DECADE I LEARNED THE FARM. I PLANTED, TENDED, HARVESTED. I CARED FOR THE ANIMALS - COWS, PIGS, HORSES AND POULTRY. I FIXED THE MACHINERY. MY FATHER SAID A HUNDRED TIMES THAT I COULD DO MORE WORK THAN ANY MAN, AND I KNEW HE WAS RIGHT ABOUT THAT! I THOUGHT MEN OUGHT NOT TO GET MORE WAGES THAN WOMEN, WHO I COULD SEE WORKED JUST AS HARD OR MORESO!

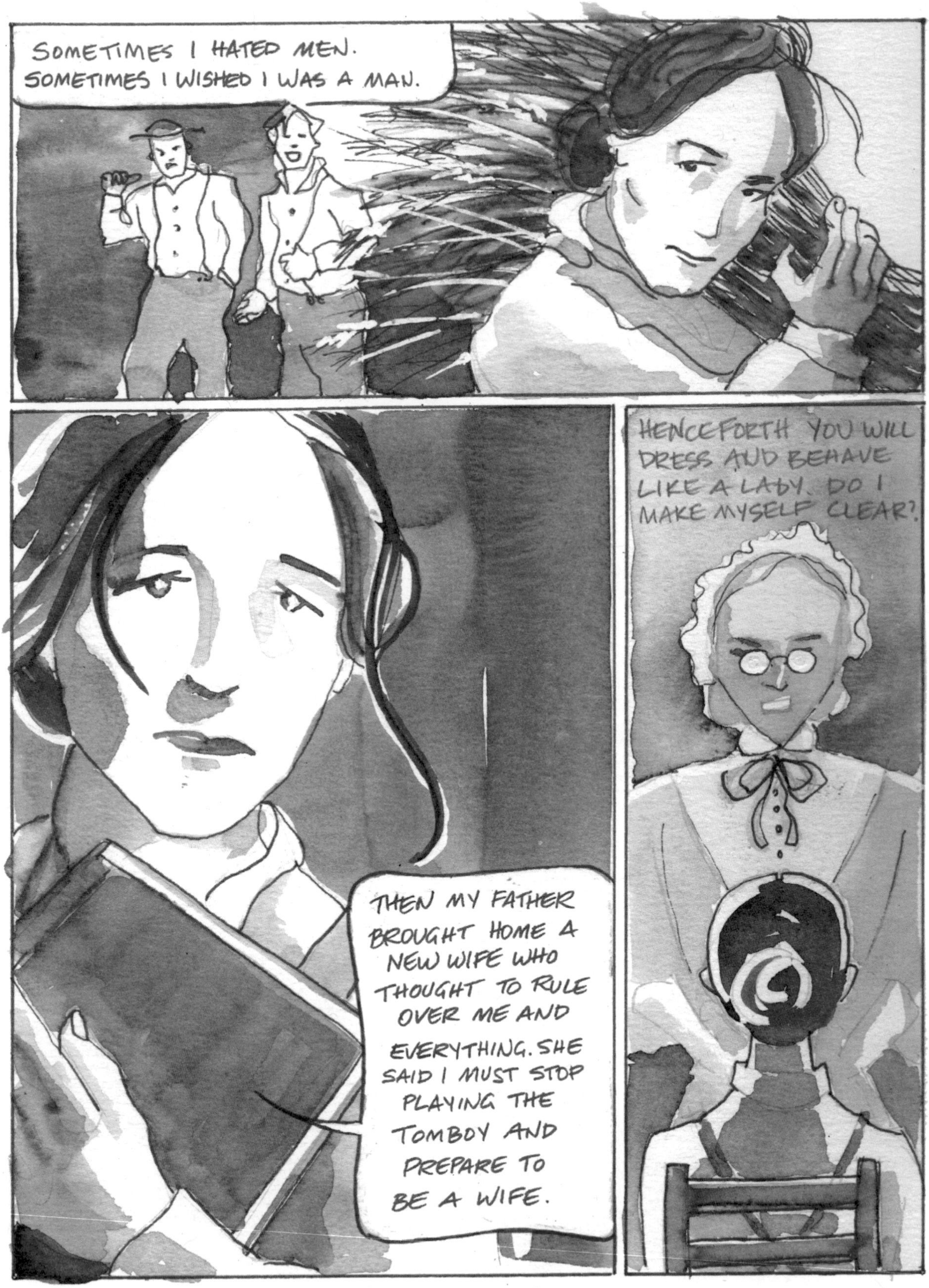
SOMETIMES I HATED MEN. SOMETIMES I WISHED I WAS A MAN.
THEN MY FATHER BROUGHT HOME A NEW WIFE WHO THOUGHT TO RULE OVER ME AND EVERYTHING. SHE SAID I MUST STOP PLAYING THE TOMBOY AND PREPARE TO BE A WIFE.
HENCEFORTH YOU WILL DRESS AND BEHAVE LIKE A LADY. DO I MAKE MYSELF CLEAR?

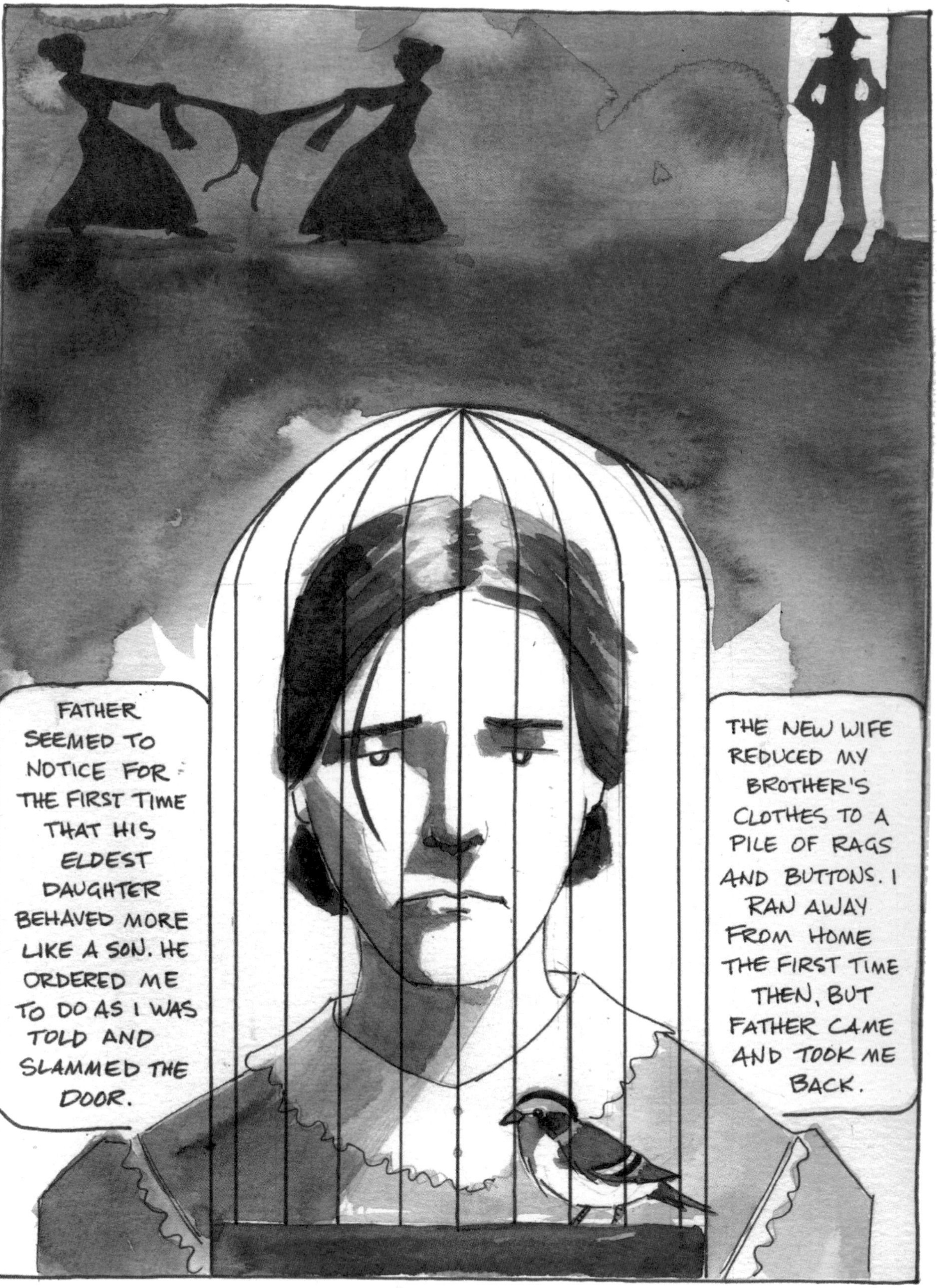
FATHER SEEMED TO NOTICE FOR THE FIRST TIME THAT HIS ELDEST DAUGHTER BEHAVED MORE LIKE A SON. HE ORDERED ME TO DO AS I WAS TOLD AND SLAMMED THE DOOR.
THE NEW WIFE REDUCED MY BROTHER'S CLOTHES TO A PILE OF RAGS AND BUTTONS. I RAN AWAY FROM HOME THE FIRST TIME THEN, BUT FATHER CAME AND TOOK ME BACK.

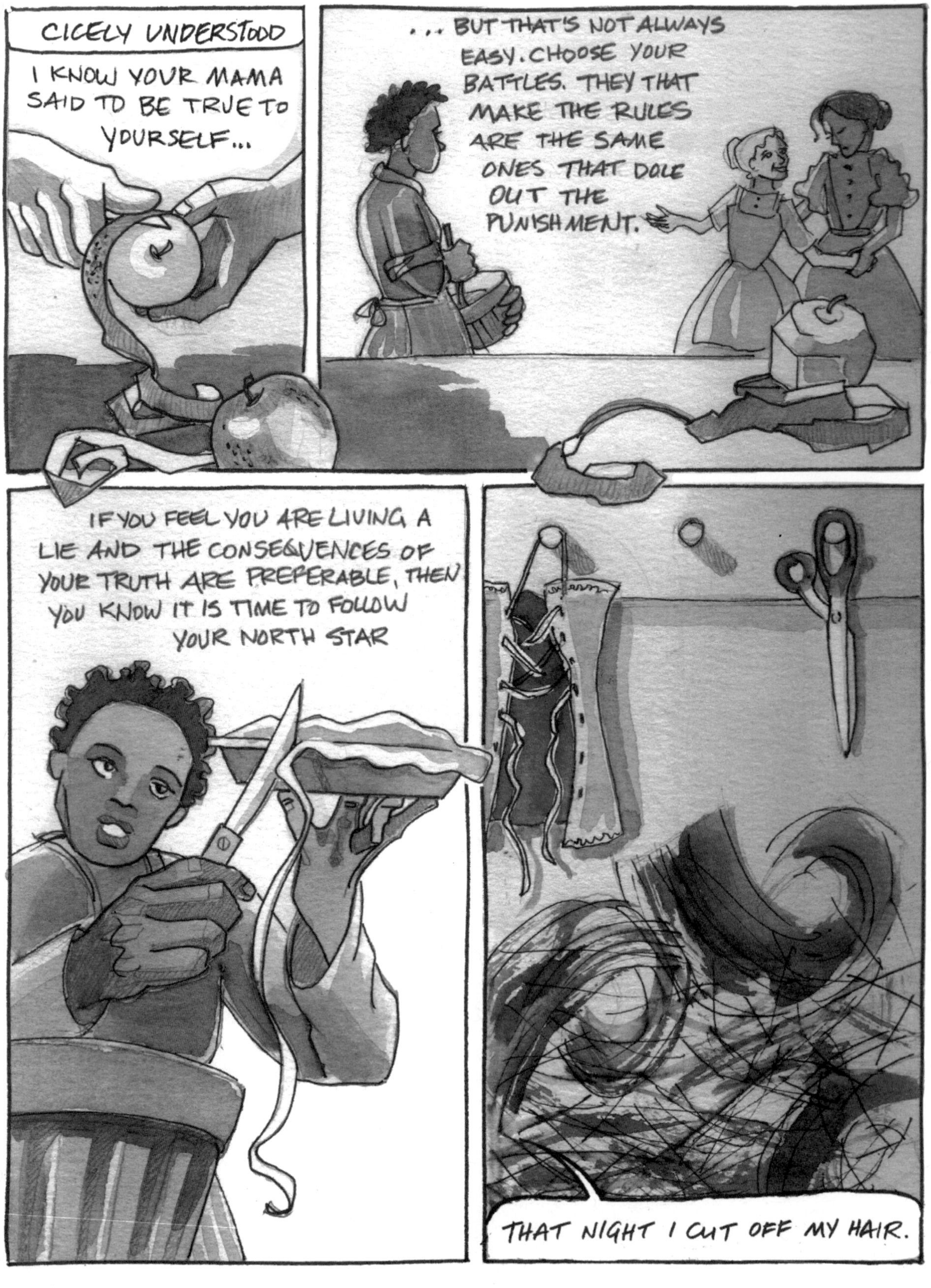
CICELY UNDERSTOOD
I KNOW YOUR MAMA SAID TO BE TRUE TO YOURSELF...
... BUT THAT'S NOT ALWAYS EASY. CHOOSE YOUR BATTLES. THEY THAT MAKE THE RULES ARE THE SAME ONES THAT DOLE OUT THE PUNISHMENT.
IF YOU FEEL YOU ARE LIVING A LIE AND THE CONSEQUENCES OF YOUR TRUTH ARE PREFERABLE, THEN YOU KNOW IT IS TIME TO FOLLOW YOUR NORTH STAR
THAT NIGHT I CUT OFF MY HAIR.

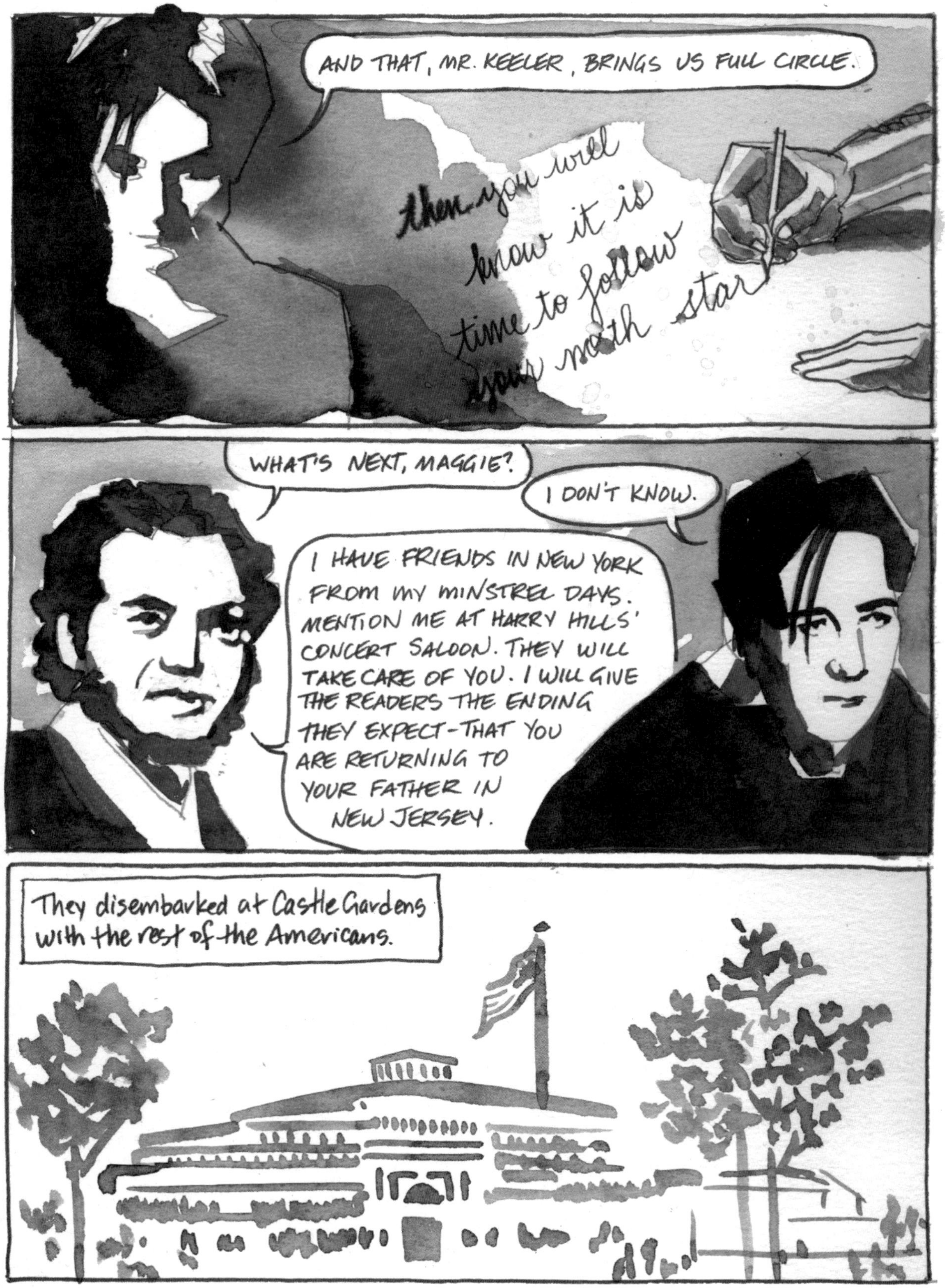
AND THAT, MR. KEELER, BRINGS US FULL CIRCLE.
then you will know it is time to follow your north star
WHAT'S NEXT, MAGGIE?
I DON'T KNOW.
I HAVE FRIENDS IN NEW YORK FROM MY MINSTREL DAYS. MENTION ME AT HARRY HILLS' CONCERT SALOON. THEY WILL TAKE CARE OF YOU. I WILL GIVE THE READERS THE ENDING THEY EXPECT-THAT YOU ARE RETURNING TO YOUR FATHER IN NEW JERSEY.
They disembarked at Castle Gardens with the rest of the Americans.

February 14, 1873

To the Editor of the Tribune:

SIR: The new steamer Victoria of the Anchor Line, which arrived at New York to-day from Glasgow, brought back to her native shores Maggie alias Billy Armstrong. She has served before the mast in several British ships. Her sex having been at last discovered, she found herself at Glasgow, and in petticoats again, about the time the Victoria was to sail. As an old sailor had gone to the shipping master of the port, and he brought her case before the managers of the Anchor Line, who gave her a free passage home. During the passage we have had many conversations with our romantic fellow-traveler, and I subjoin an account of her story as far as possible in her own words. She is 19 years old, of medium size, with a play of humor about her eyes that partially redeems the plainness of her determined, somewhat masculine face. So high has she held female virtue through all her vicissitudes that when a steerage passenger of the Victoria insulted a woman in her presence, two or three days ago, she very calmly struck out from the shoulder and knocked him down.

"My name," she says, "is Maggie Armstrong, though I called myself Billy when I put on pantaloons. I was born in the State of New Jersey, America. My father is a farmer five miles from Trenton, and he has told me hundreds of times that I could do more work than any man. I was always of a wild, passionate nature. I used to hate men, when I was at home. I thought they ought not to get more wages than women, and I often wished I was a man. My mother died eight years ago, and left another little sister and me. Father kept a housekeeper until I was able to do his work, which I did till the first of last April, when he took a notion to get married. This new wife he got in New York. She came to our house and thought to rule me and everything; but I soon taught her her mistake. I left the house and went and hired out at a neighboring farmer's. My father came after me and took me home, and I stayed eight days leading a cat-and-dog life with my stepmother. I thought I could not endure that long, so I took a strange notion into my head. I was up stairs one day along with one of my schoolmates. I was engaged cleaning and folding my

father's clothes, and I said to her that if I was to dress myself in his clothes he would have a job to find me. She laughed, and said he would. There was silence between us for a few minutes, and without saying anything more about it to her I secretly determined to try it. At 2 o'clock that night, or the next morning I mean, I went up stairs and dressed myself in my father's clothes. I took the scissors and cut my hair as short as I could, and then went down stairs again and took $25 out of one of the bureau-drawers, for I knew it was no use going away without money. Then I went to the station and took the 4:20 train for New York. I wandered about the city a good deal, stopping at a small hotel in Warren street, I think. I hadn't begun to make up my mind what to do, for I had never been in New York before, when one of those runners hailed me and wanted me to ship on a freight steamer, which he said was going to London and back to New York in a month. That seemed to suit me, as I was curious to see London. He shipped me as engineer's steward. I never was sea sick once – in fact, I never was so well before in my life as I have been at sea. I always used to have Jersey headaches in the summer time at home. No more feverishness now. All the engineers were very well pleased with my work. But they informed me that the ship was not going back to New York, but to China, when she left London. So I was discharged at my own request in London, the head engineer presenting me with ten shillings for being a good, clean lad. With this and my wages, 15 shillings, and what was left of my $25, I was enabled to live in London for three weeks. I went all over the great city and saw no end of things. As soon as I learned that the steamer was going to China, I made up my mind that I had to get back to America as a sailor, if I ever got back at all. So I used during my spare hours on the steamer, to practice going aloft; or if they were stowing sails or doing anything of the kind, I was sure to be on hand. I used to go into the wheel-house, too, and learn to steer, and before I got to the Banks of Newfoundland I knew all the compass.

"When, therefore I shipped on board the bark Princess, bound for Middlesboro, it was not as an apprentice, but as an ordinary seaman, for two pounds five shilling a month. I had bought a sailor's chest and recruited my sailor's wardrobe

with a set of oil-skins. These I had taken from the Sailor's Home boarding-house to the forecastle of the Princess, and my life as a common tar began. There were only eight of us in the forecastle, and as I was always first to reef the topsails and furl the small sails in a gale of wind, we got along very well. I was discharged, finally, with the rest at Middlesboro' after a three weeks' run. Then I thought I should like to see Shields, which is only six miles distant. I went there and tried to ship again; but here arose a great difficulty. Unfortunately, I had lost my discharge. The captain of a bark, the Eskdale of Whitby, bound for Italy, would take me as an apprentice, but not as an ordinary seaman – that is, not at first, for he did take me when he found that he could not get any apprentices. We left Shields loaded with coal for Genoa. We had headwinds and bad weather in the English Channel, but the Mediterranean was fair enough to make up for it. We were in Genoa nine weeks in all, and it was after we had been there six weeks that I was found out not to be a man. It happened in this way: There was a brute of a sailor in the forecastle, who was always imposing on me; when we were shoveling coal in the hold he made me fill two baskets to his one; I was telling this to the rest of the crew after were done work; he gave me the lie, and the result was a knock-down fight between us; he was the bigger and he got the better of me, and I began crying. This led to suspicions of my sex. I stoutly maintained that I was a man, but it was no use. Now the captain's wife was on board, and to him and her I was at last forced to confess my whole story. I was soon habited as a woman again and engaged as a stewardess in the cabin for the homeward run. Stopping some weeks at Malaga for a cargo the bark landed finally at Aberdeen, whence I came by train to Glasgow."

During the passage from Glasgow to New York the hero and heroine of the foregoing story has conducted herself in a quiet, modest way – except in the matter of knocking down a steerage passenger for insulting a woman; and, as for that, you never saw a quieter or modester knockdown in your life. Maggie starts at once for New Jersey and her father.

RALPH KEELER

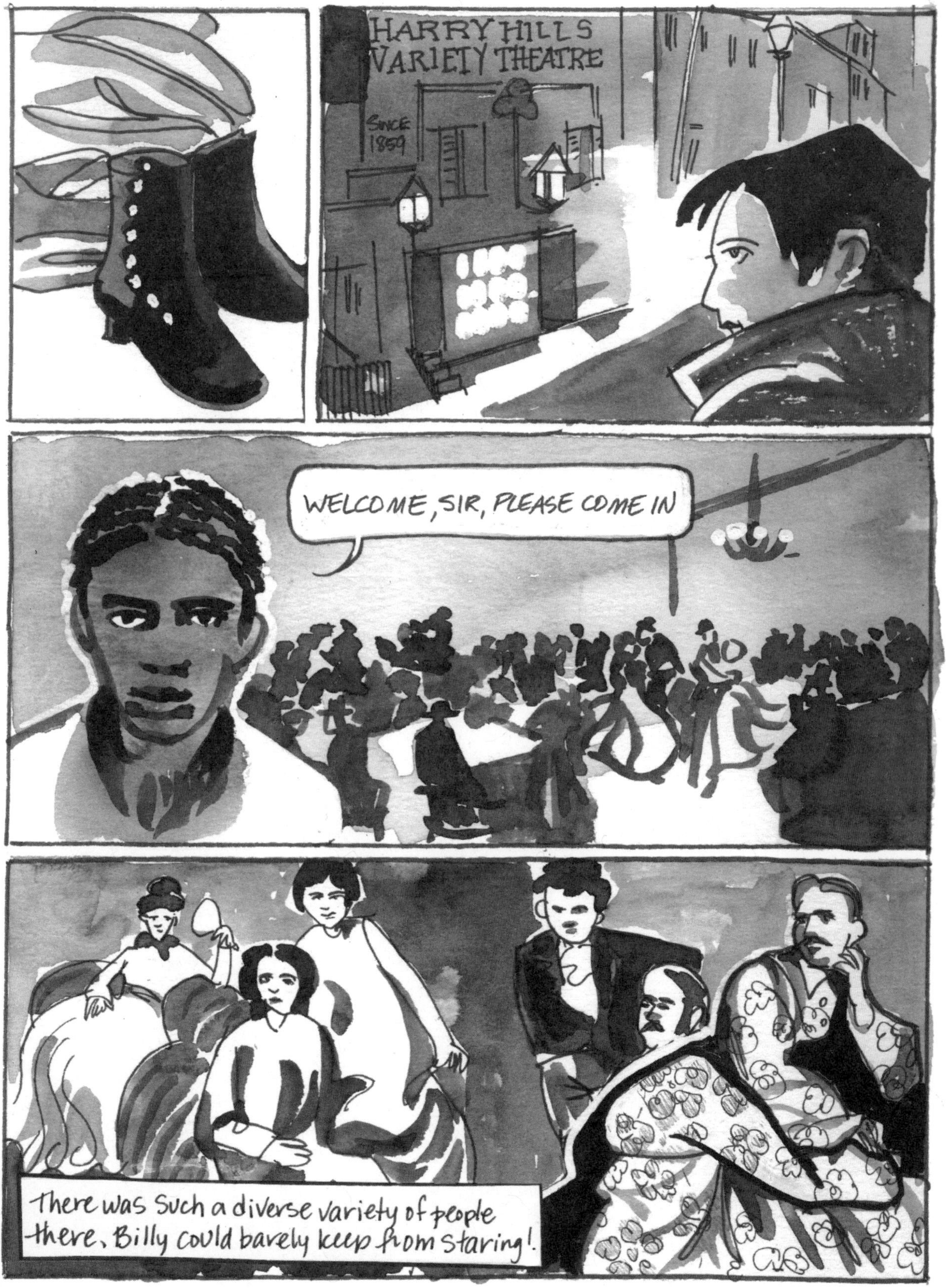
HARRY HILLS
VARIETY THEATRE
SINCE
1859
WELCOME, SIR, PLEASE COME IN
There was such a diverse variety of people there. Billy could barely keep from staring!

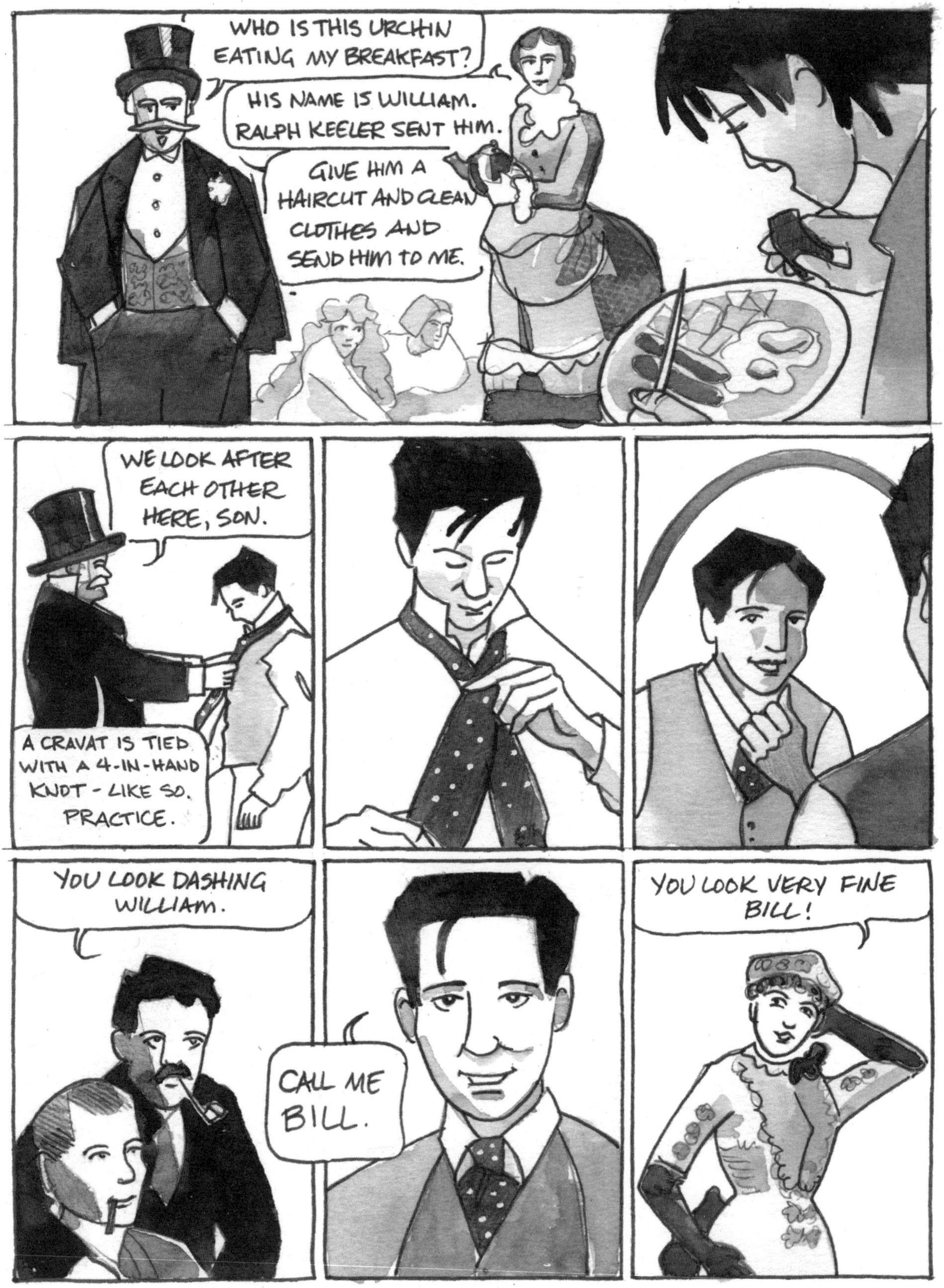
WHO IS THIS URCHIN EATING MY BREAKFAST?
HIS NAME IS WILLIAM. RALPH KEELER SENT HIM.
GIVE HIM A HAIRCUT AND CLEAN CLOTHES AND SEND HIM TO ME.
WE LOOK AFTER EACH OTHER HERE, SON.
A CRAVAT IS TIED WITH A 4-IN-HAND KNOT - LIKE SO. PRACTICE.
YOU LOOK DASHING WILLIAM.
CALL ME BILL.
YOU LOOK VERY FINE BILL!

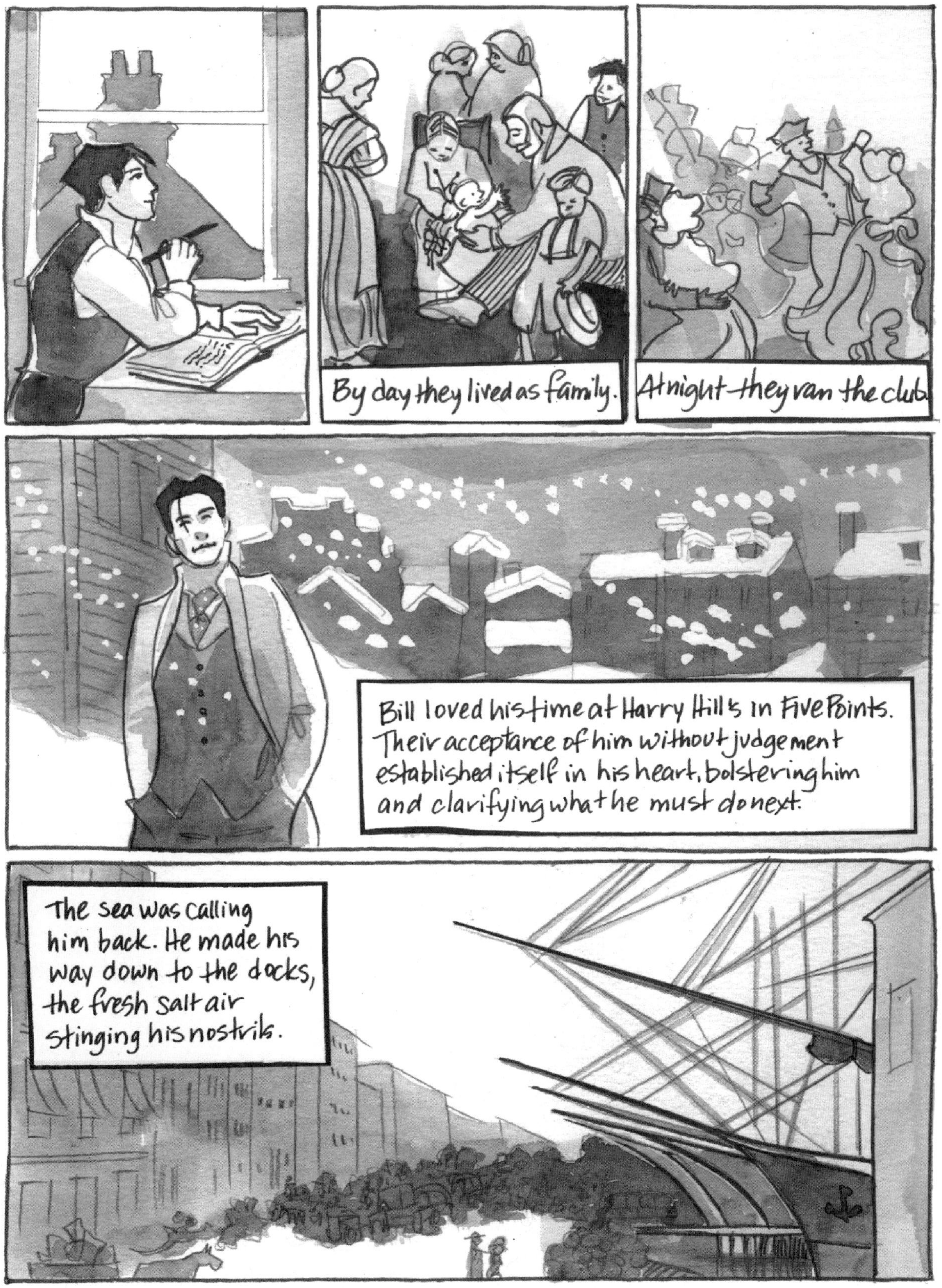
By day they lived as family.
At night they ran the club
Bill loved his time at Harry Hill's in Five Points. Their acceptance of him without judgement established itself in his heart, bolstering him and clarifying what he must do next.
The sea was calling him back. He made his way down to the docks, the fresh salt air stinging his nostrils.

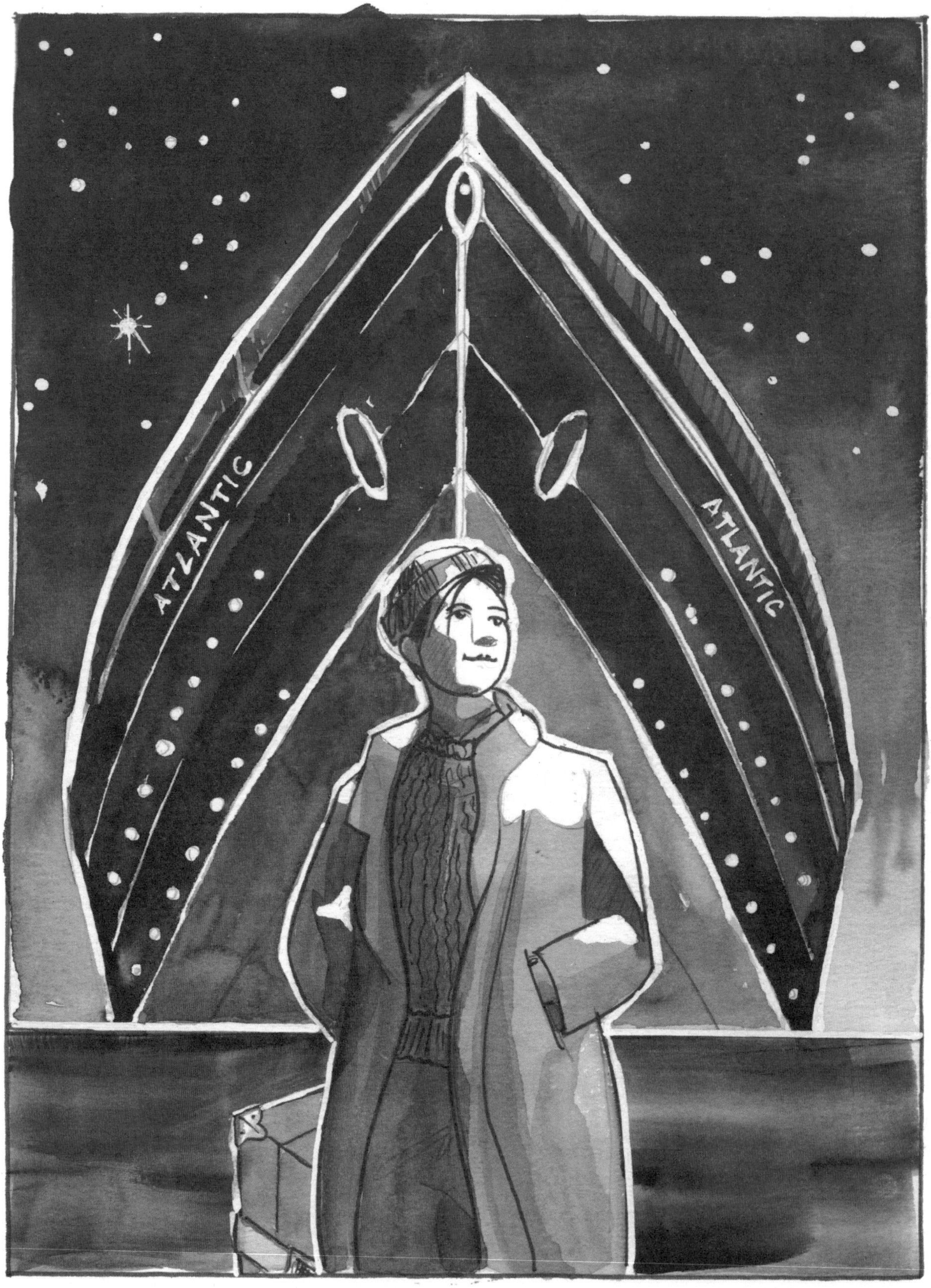
ATLANTIC
ATLANTIC

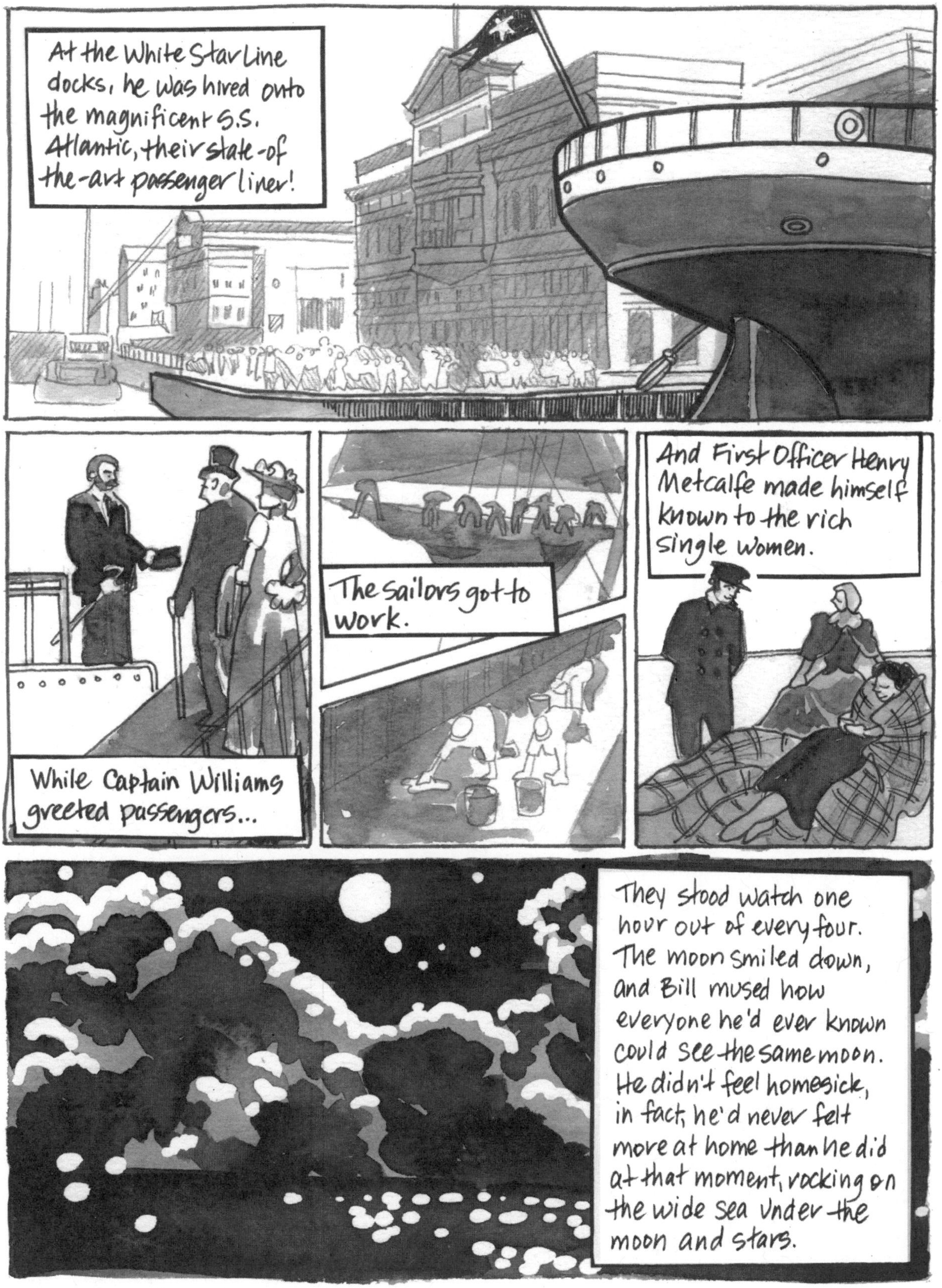
At the White Star Line docks, he was hired onto the magnificent S.S. Atlantic, their state-of the-art passenger liner!
While Captain Williams greeted passengers...
The sailors got to work.
And First Officer Henry Metcalfe made himself known to the rich single women.
They stood watch one hour out of every four. The moon smiled down, and Bill mused how everyone he'd ever known could see the same moon. He didn't feel homesick, in fact, he'd never felt more at home than he did at that moment, rocking on the wide sea under the moon and stars.

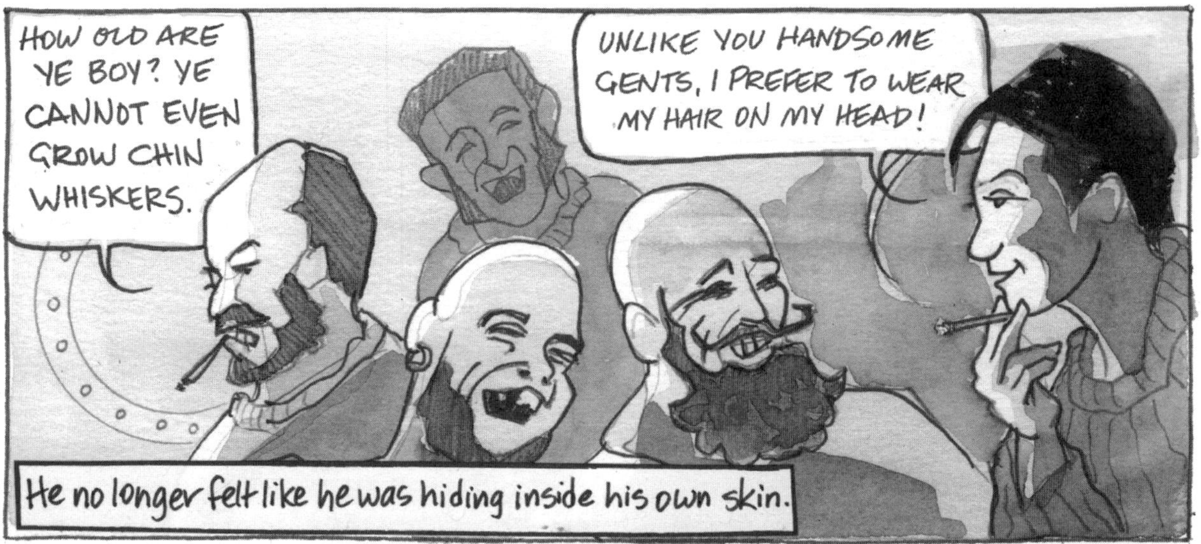
HOW OLD ARE YE BOY? YE CANNOT EVEN GROW CHIN WHISKERS.
UNLIKE YOU HANDSOME GENTS, I PREFER TO WEAR MY HAIR ON MY HEAD!
He no longer felt like he was hiding inside his own skin.

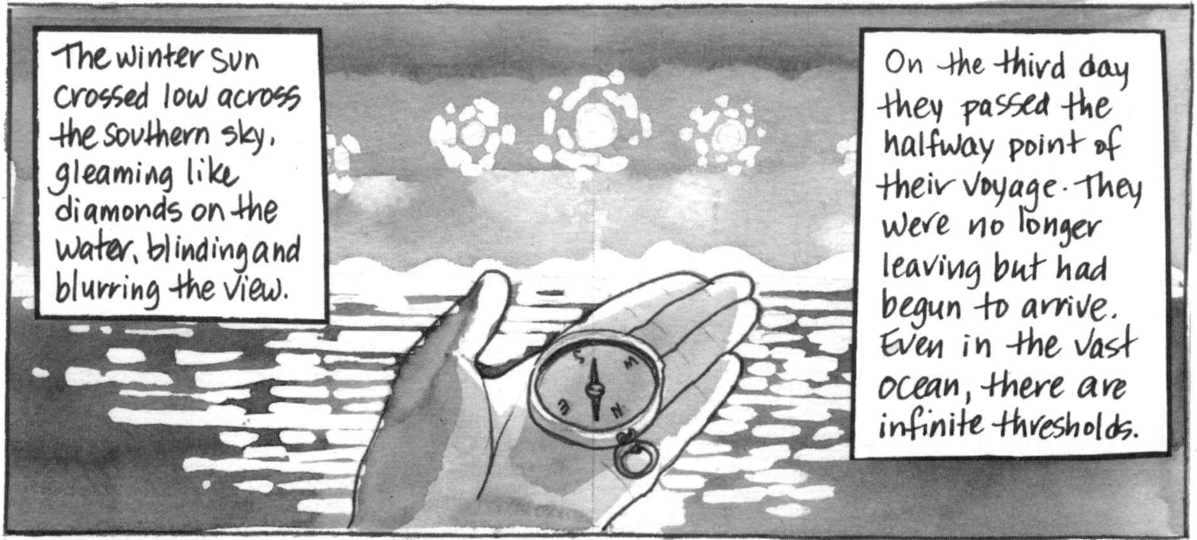
The winter sun crossed low across the southern sky, gleaming like diamonds on the water, blinding and blurring the view.
On the third day they passed the halfway point of their voyage. They were no longer leaving but had begun to arrive. Even in the vast ocean, there are infinite thresholds.

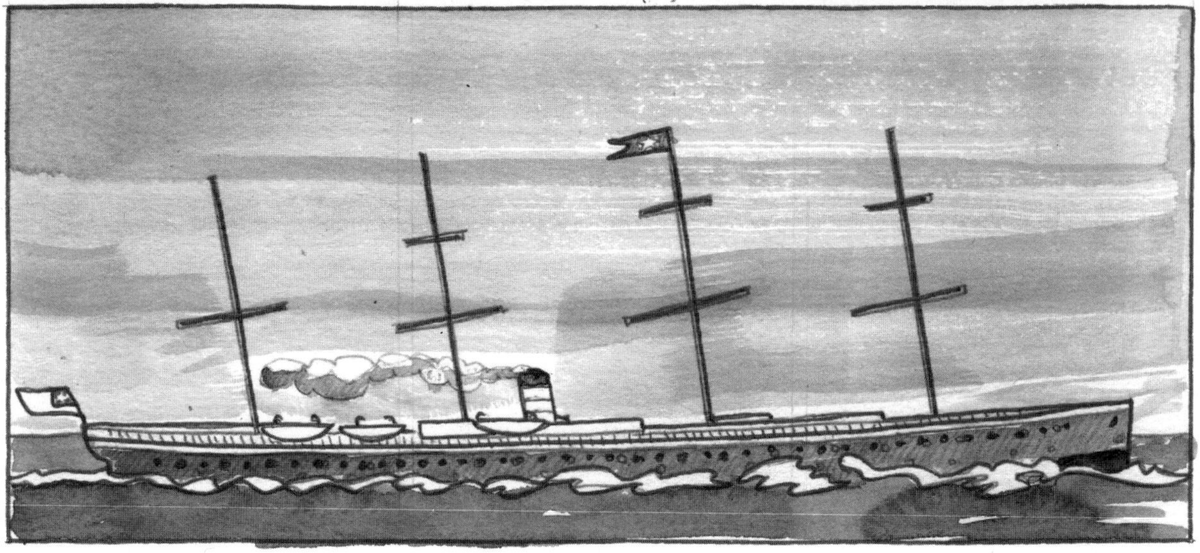

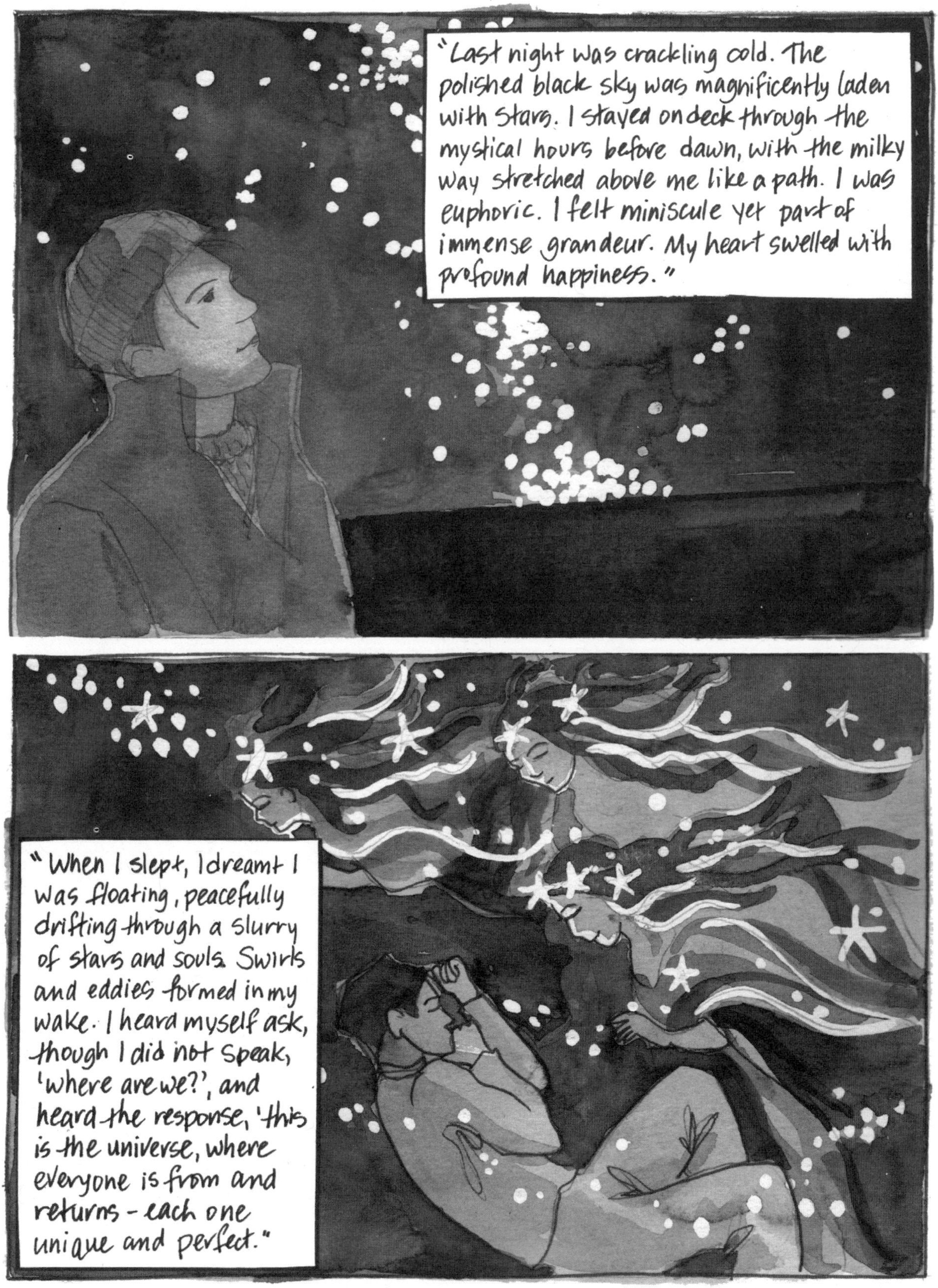
"Last night was crackling cold. The polished black sky was magnificently laden with stars. I stayed on deck through the mystical hours before dawn, with the milky way stretched above me like a path. I was euphoric. I felt miniscule yet part of immense grandeur. My heart swelled with profound happiness."
"When I slept, I dreamt I was floating, peacefully drifting through a slurry of stars and souls. Swirls and eddies formed in my wake. I heard myself ask, though I did not speak, 'where are we?', and heard the response, 'this is the universe, where everyone is from and returns - each one unique and perfect.'"

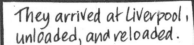

They arrived at Liverpool, unloaded, and reloaded.

WELCOME ABOARD!

ATLANTIC

I AM CAPTAIN JAMES WILLIAMS. I HOPE YOU HAVE A VERY PLEASANT JOURNEY ABOARD THE S.S. ATLANTIC!

They steamed to Ireland and took on more passengers, cargo and mail.

While the passengers attended the morning church service, the crew practiced lifeboat drills.

C'MON BILL. YE'LL SOON HAVE PLENTY OF TIME TO MOP UP PUKE.

Quartermaster Thomas wasn't wrong!

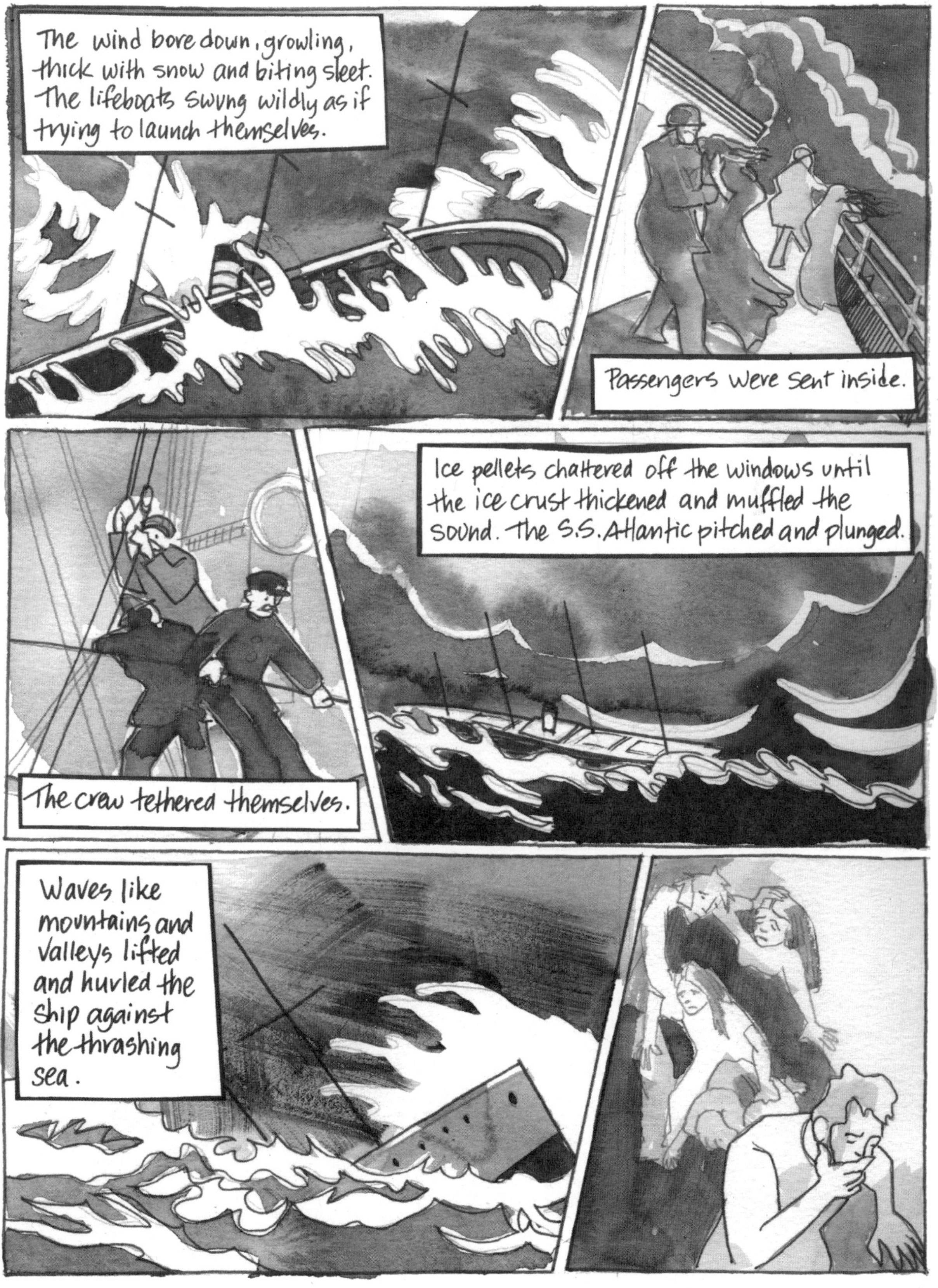
The wind bore down, growling, thick with snow and biting sleet. The lifeboats swung wildly as if trying to launch themselves.
Passengers were sent inside.
The crew tethered themselves.
Ice pellets chattered off the windows until the ice crust thickened and muffled the sound. The S.S. Atlantic pitched and plunged.
Waves like mountains and valleys lifted and hurled the ship against the thrashing sea.

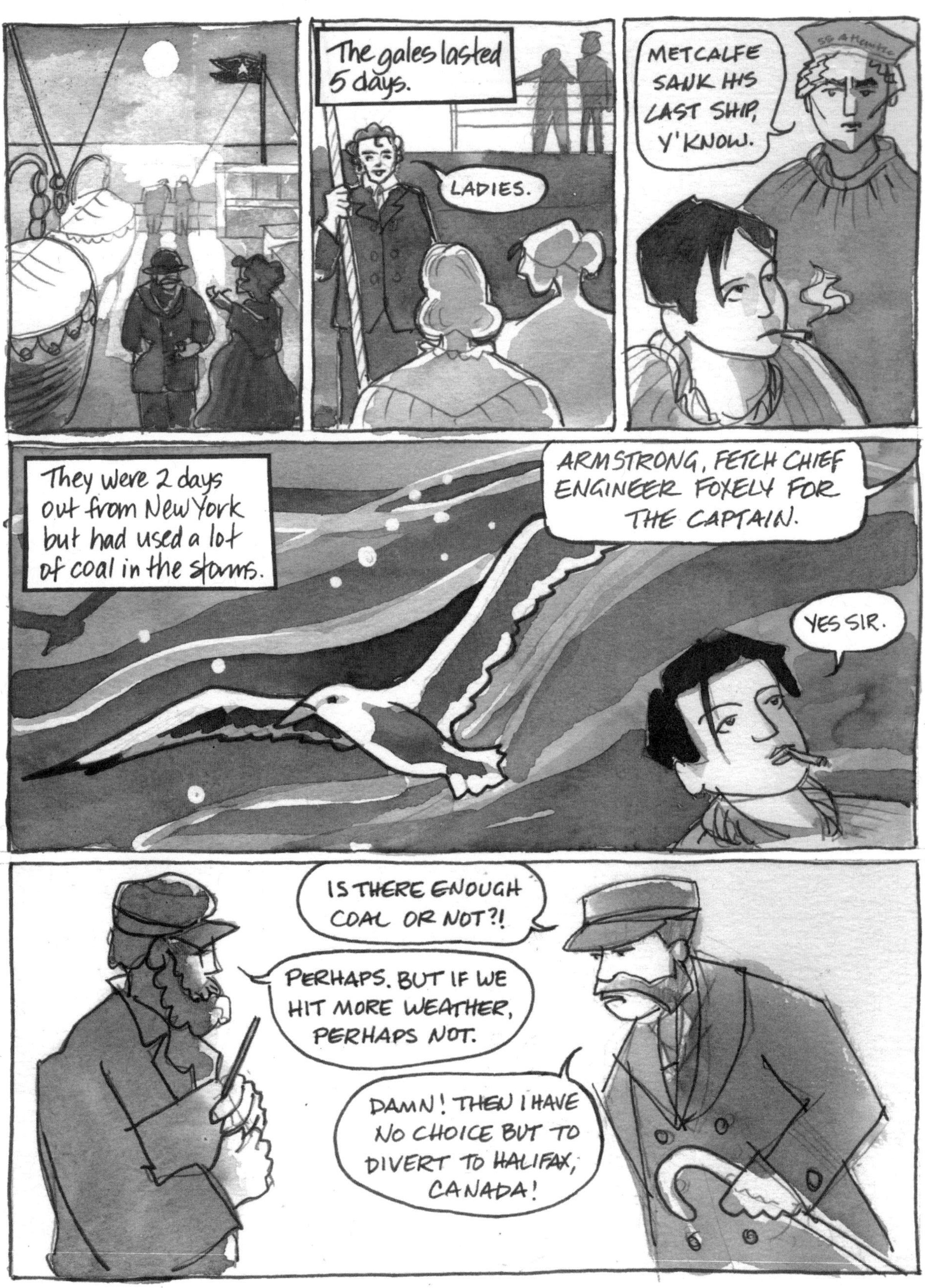
The gales lasted 5 days.
LADIES.
METCALFE SANK HIS LAST SHIP, Y'KNOW.
They were 2 days out from New York but had used a lot of coal in the storms.
ARMSTRONG, FETCH CHIEF ENGINEER FOXELY FOR THE CAPTAIN.
YES SIR.
IS THERE ENOUGH COAL OR NOT?!
PERHAPS. BUT IF WE HIT MORE WEATHER, PERHAPS NOT.
DAMN! THEN I HAVE NO CHOICE BUT TO DIVERT TO HALIFAX, CANADA!

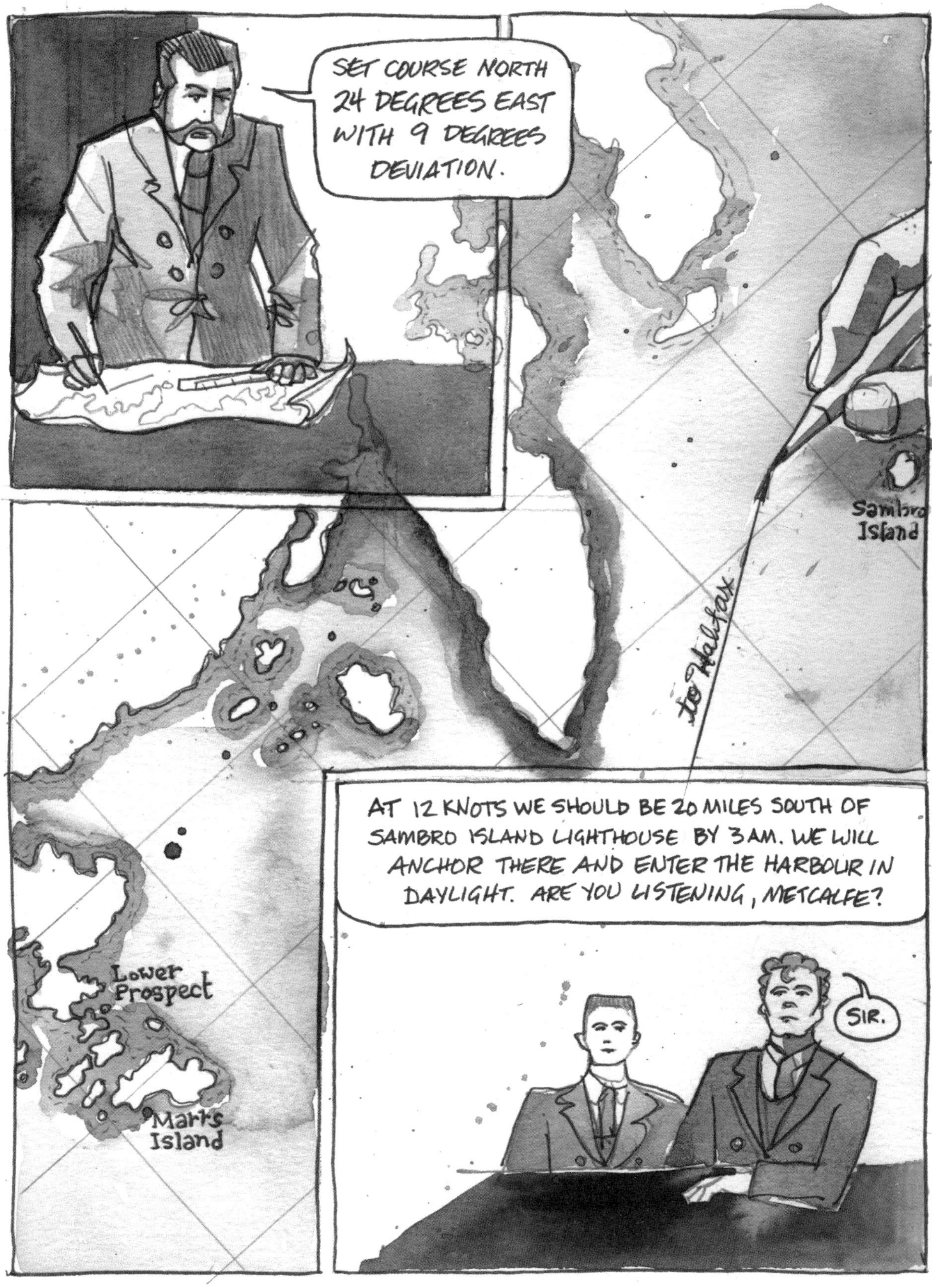

SET COURSE NORTH 24 DEGREES EAST WITH 9 DEGREES DEVIATION.
Sambro Island
to Halifax
Lower Prospect
Mars Island
AT 12 KNOTS WE SHOULD BE 20 MILES SOUTH OF SAMBRO ISLAND LIGHTHOUSE BY 3AM. WE WILL ANCHOR THERE AND ENTER THE HARBOUR IN DAYLIGHT. ARE YOU LISTENING, METCALFE?
SIR.

The sailors set about repairing the damage from the storms. Lamps, sails, ropes, lifeboats took a beating.

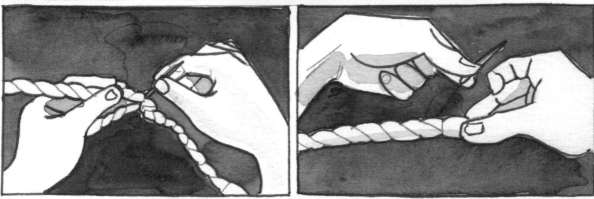

HAVE YOU BEEN TO HALIFAX, ROGER?

CAN'T SAY AS I HAVE.

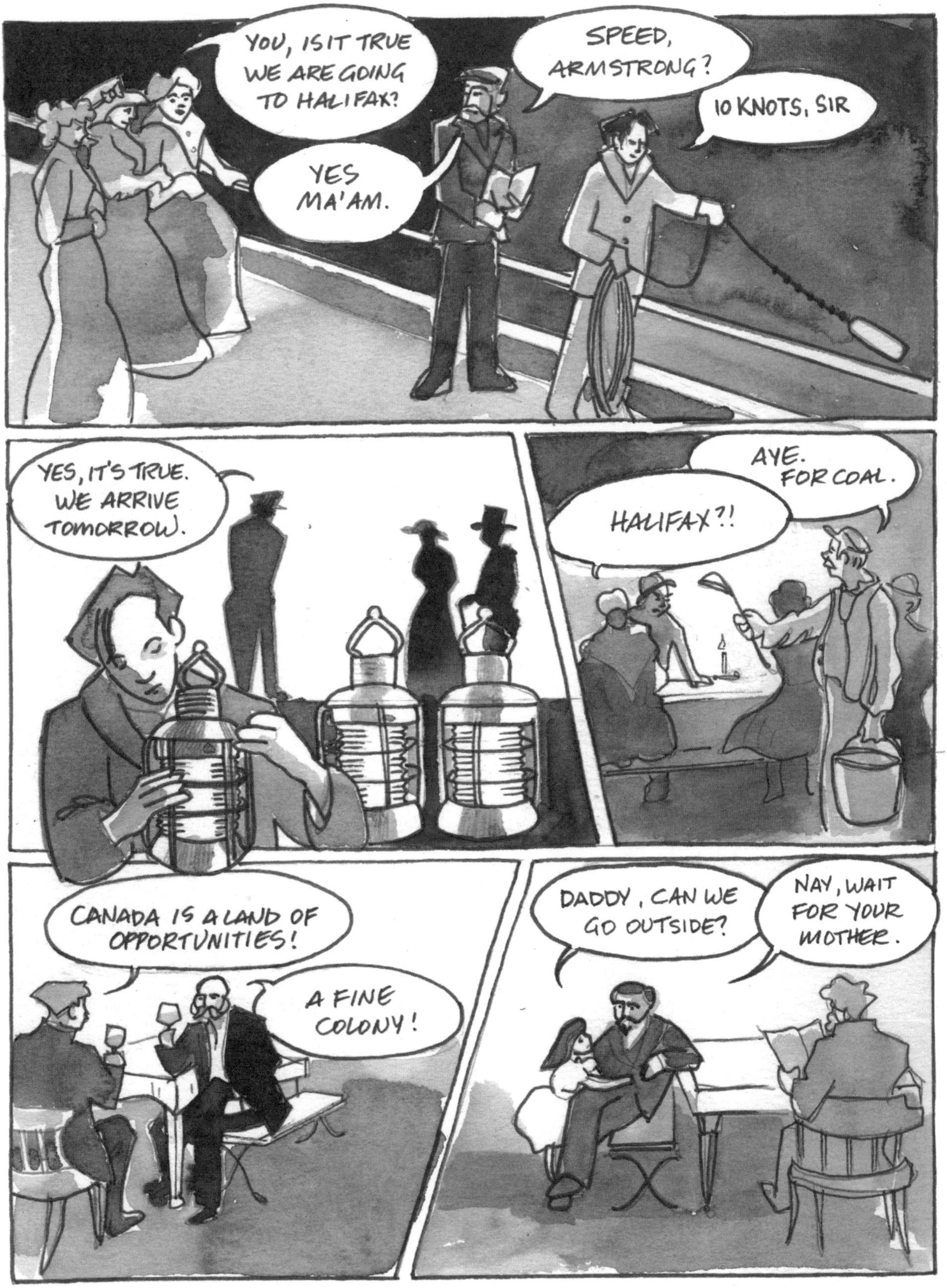

YOU, IS IT TRUE WE ARE GOING TO HALIFAX?
YES MA'AM.
SPEED, ARMSTRONG?
10 KNOTS, SIR
YES, IT'S TRUE. WE ARRIVE TOMORROW.
HALIFAX?!
AYE. FOR COAL.
CANADA IS A LAND OF OPPORTUNITIES!
A FINE COLONY!
DADDY, CAN WE GO OUTSIDE?
NAY, WAIT FOR YOUR MOTHER.

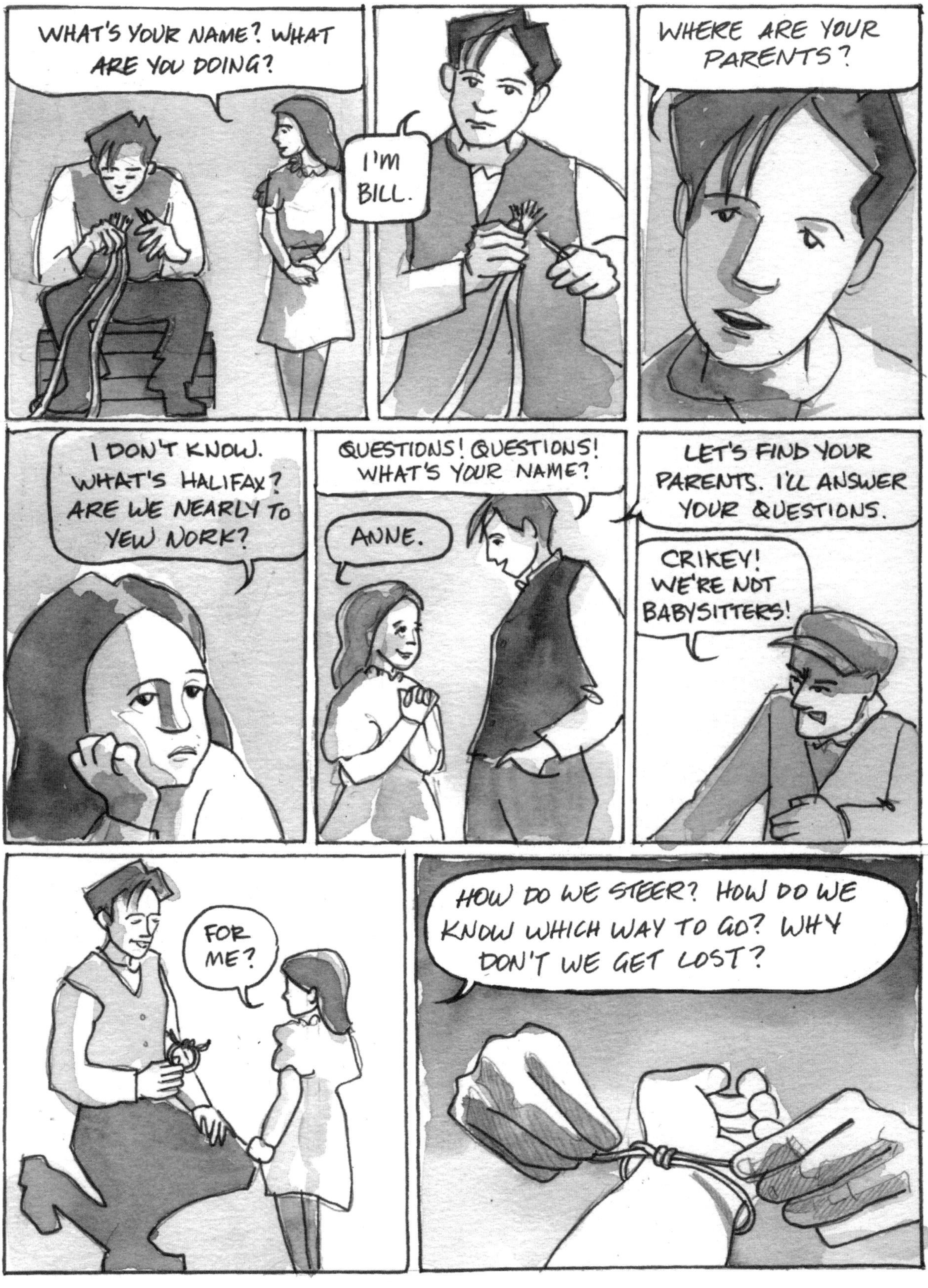
WHAT'S YOUR NAME? WHAT ARE YOU DOING?
I'M BILL.
WHERE ARE YOUR PARENTS?
I DON'T KNOW. WHAT'S HALIFAX? ARE WE NEARLY TO YEW NORK?
QUESTIONS! QUESTIONS! WHAT'S YOUR NAME?
ANNE.
LET'S FIND YOUR PARENTS. I'LL ANSWER YOUR QUESTIONS.
CRIKEY! WE'RE NOT BABYSITTERS!
FOR ME?
HOW DO WE STEER? HOW DO WE KNOW WHICH WAY TO GO? WHY DON'T WE GET LOST?

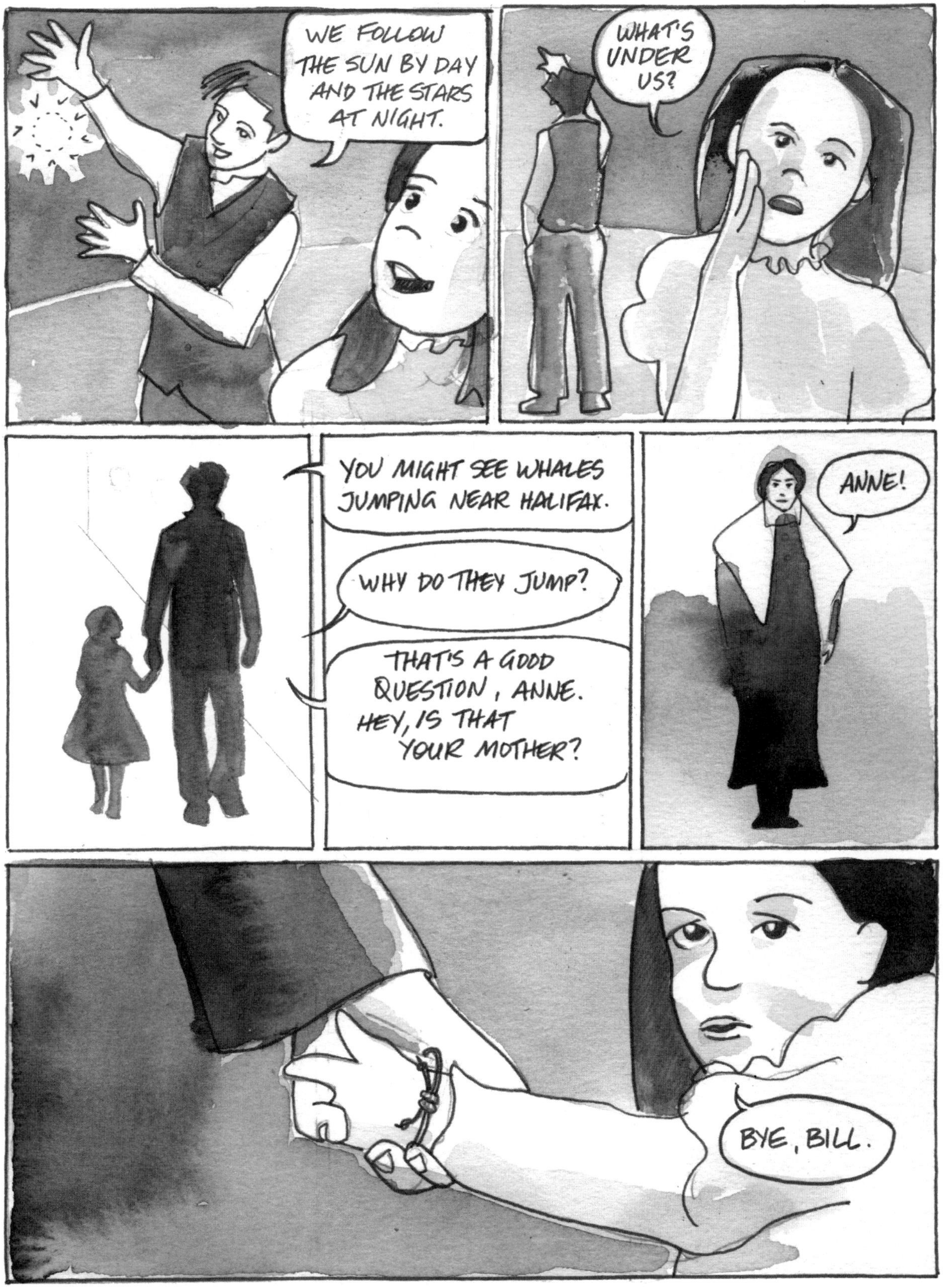
WE FOLLOW THE SUN BY DAY AND THE STARS AT NIGHT.
WHAT'S UNDER US?
YOU MIGHT SEE WHALES JUMPING NEAR HALIFAX.
WHY DO THEY JUMP?
THAT'S A GOOD QUESTION, ANNE. HEY, IS THAT YOUR MOTHER?
ANNE!
BYE, BILL.

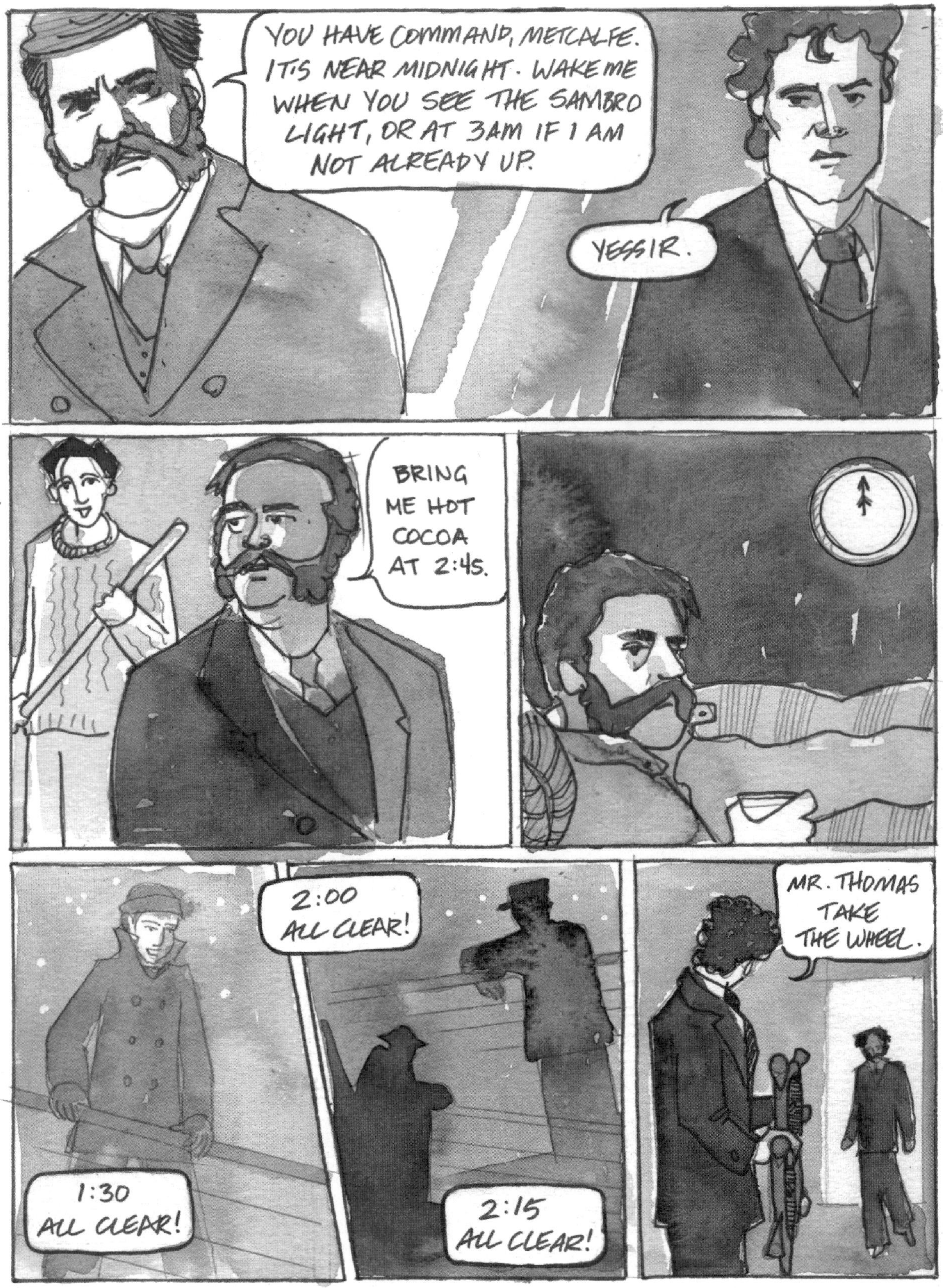
YOU HAVE COMMAND, METCALFE. IT'S NEAR MIDNIGHT. WAKE ME WHEN YOU SEE THE SAMBRO LIGHT, OR AT 3AM IF I AM NOT ALREADY UP.
YESSIR.
BRING ME HOT COCOA AT 2:45.
1:30 ALL CLEAR!
2:00 ALL CLEAR!
2:15 ALL CLEAR!
MR. THOMAS TAKE THE WHEEL.

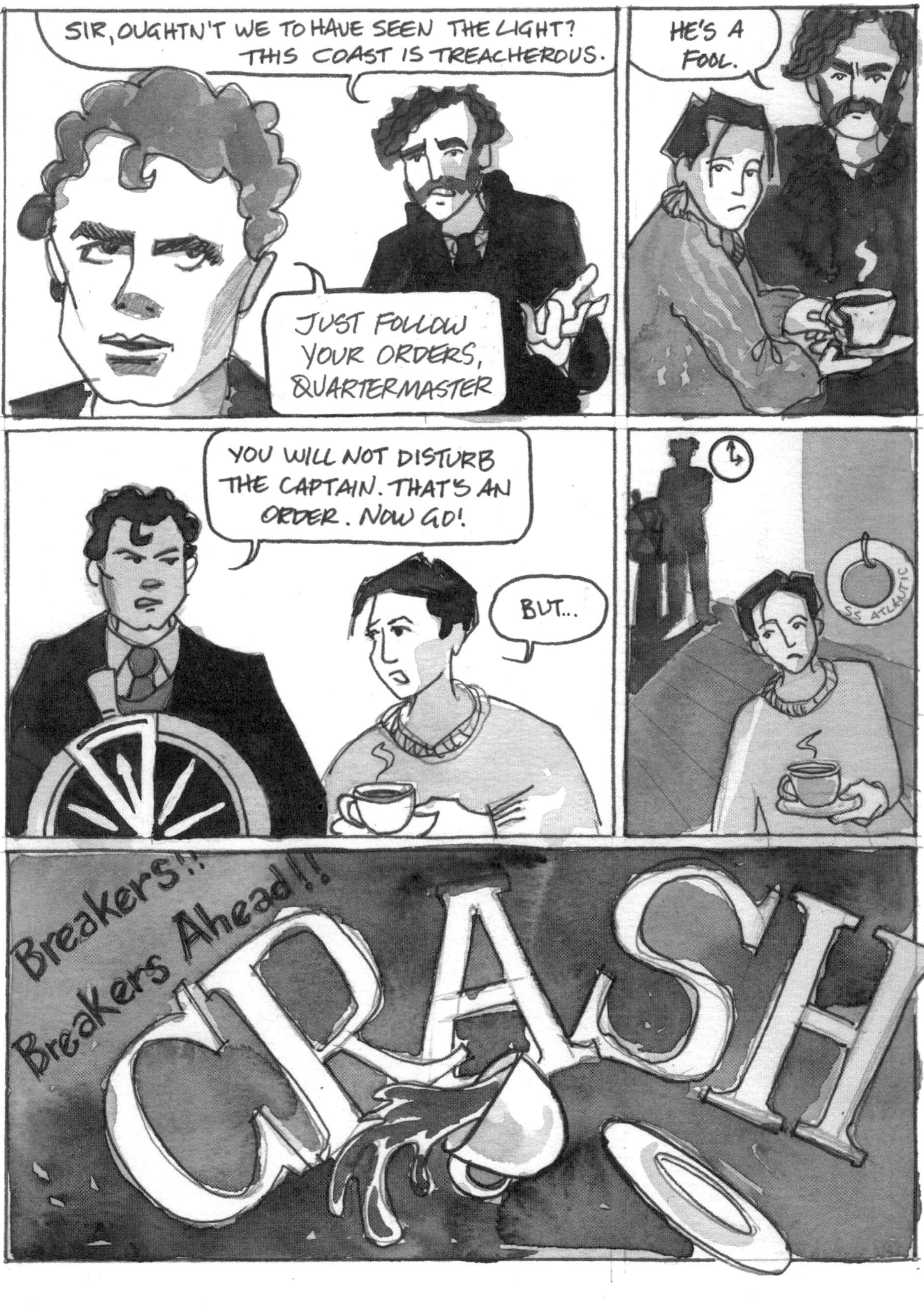
SIR, OUGHTN'T WE TO HAVE SEEN THE LIGHT? THIS COAST IS TREACHEROUS.
JUST FOLLOW YOUR ORDERS, QUARTERMASTER
HE'S A FOOL.
YOU WILL NOT DISTURB THE CAPTAIN. THAT'S AN ORDER. NOW GO!
BUT...
SS ATLANTIC
Breakers!!
Breakers Ahead!!
CRASH

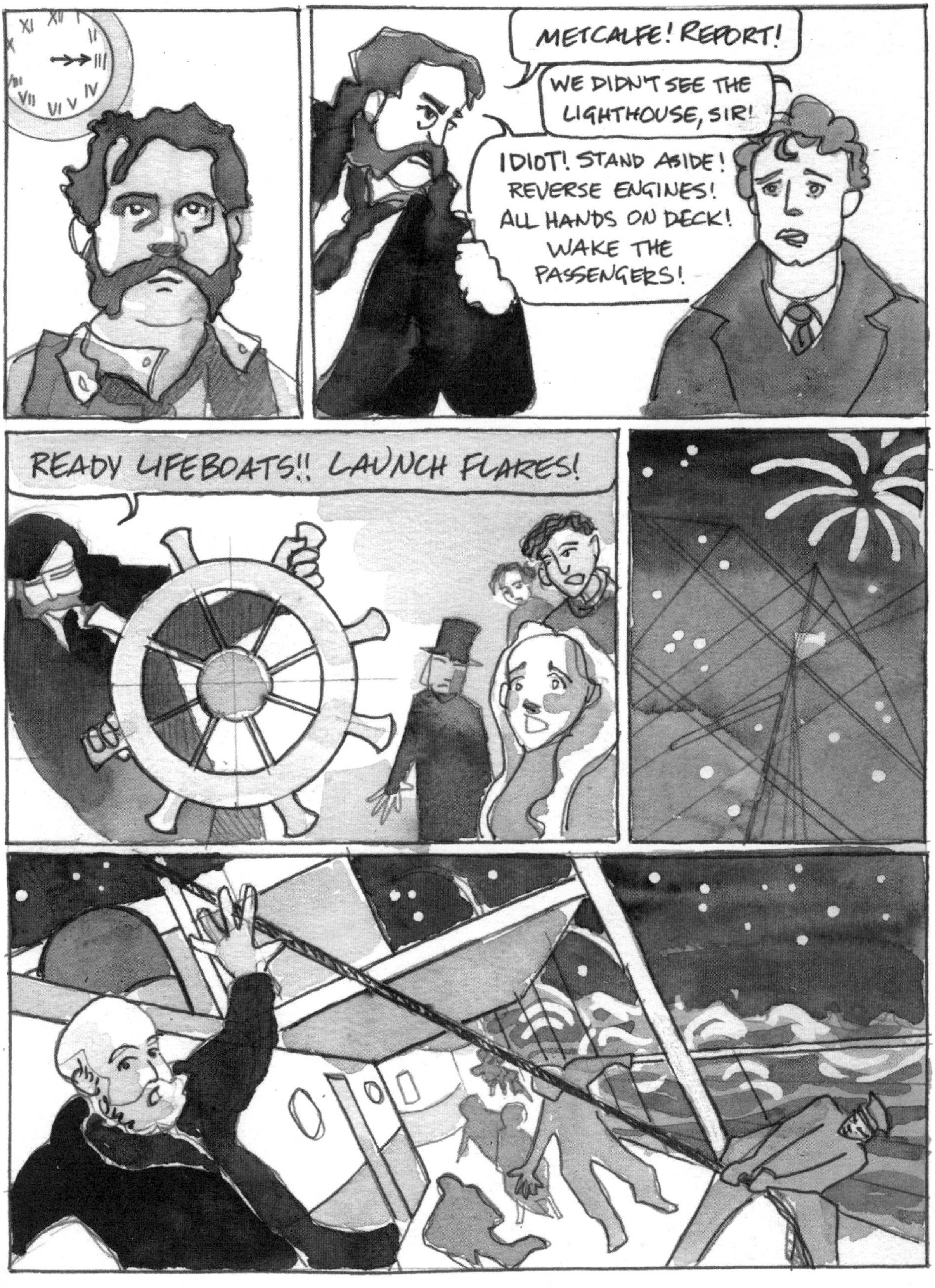
METCALFE! REPORT!
WE DIDN'T SEE THE LIGHTHOUSE, SIR!
IDIOT! STAND ASIDE! REVERSE ENGINES! ALL HANDS ON DECK! WAKE THE PASSENGERS!
READY LIFEBOATS!! LAUNCH FLARES!

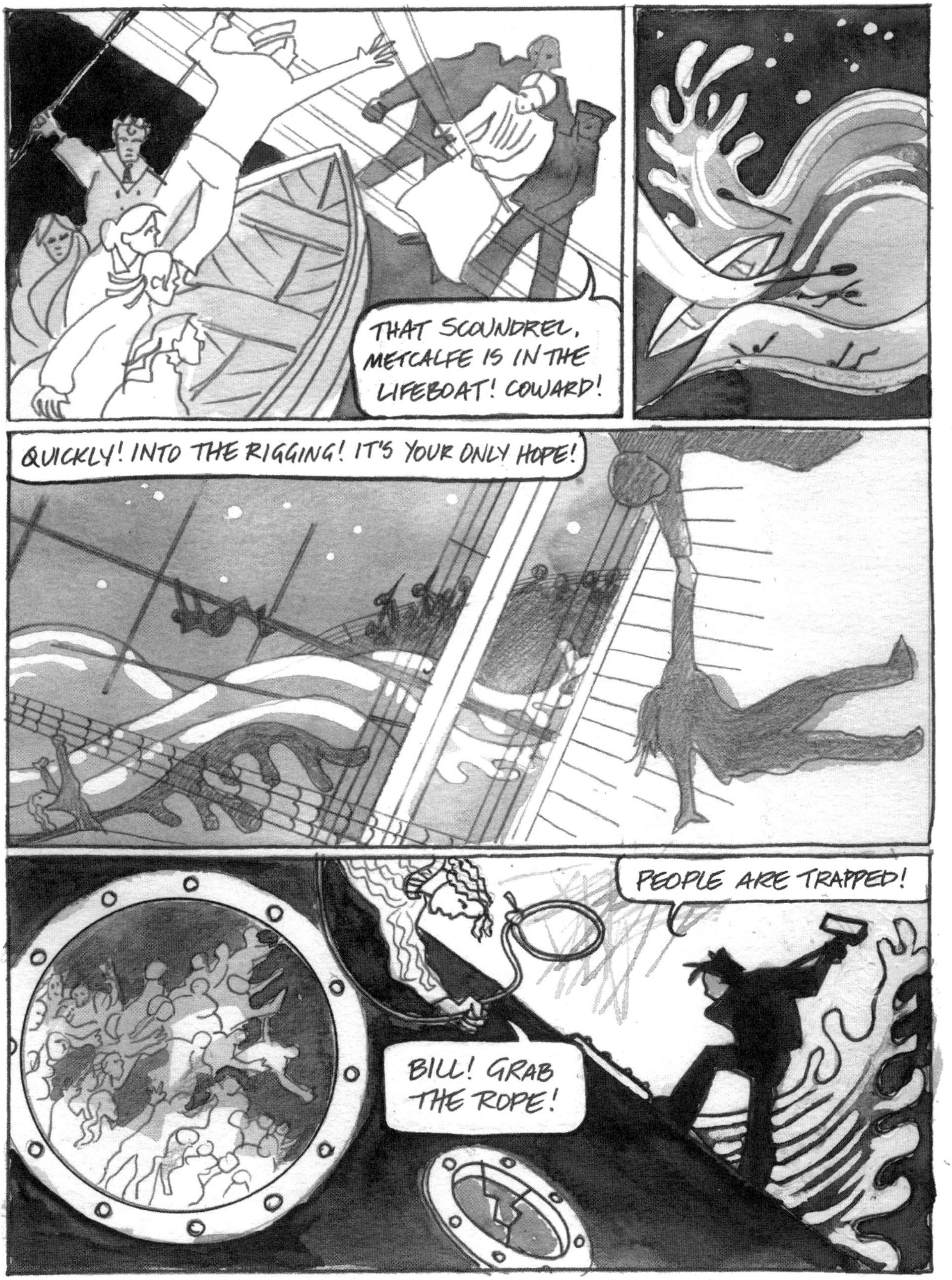
THAT SCOUNDREL, METCALFE IS IN THE LIFEBOAT! COWARD!
QUICKLY! INTO THE RIGGING! IT'S YOUR ONLY HOPE!
PEOPLE ARE TRAPPED!
BILL! GRAB THE ROPE!

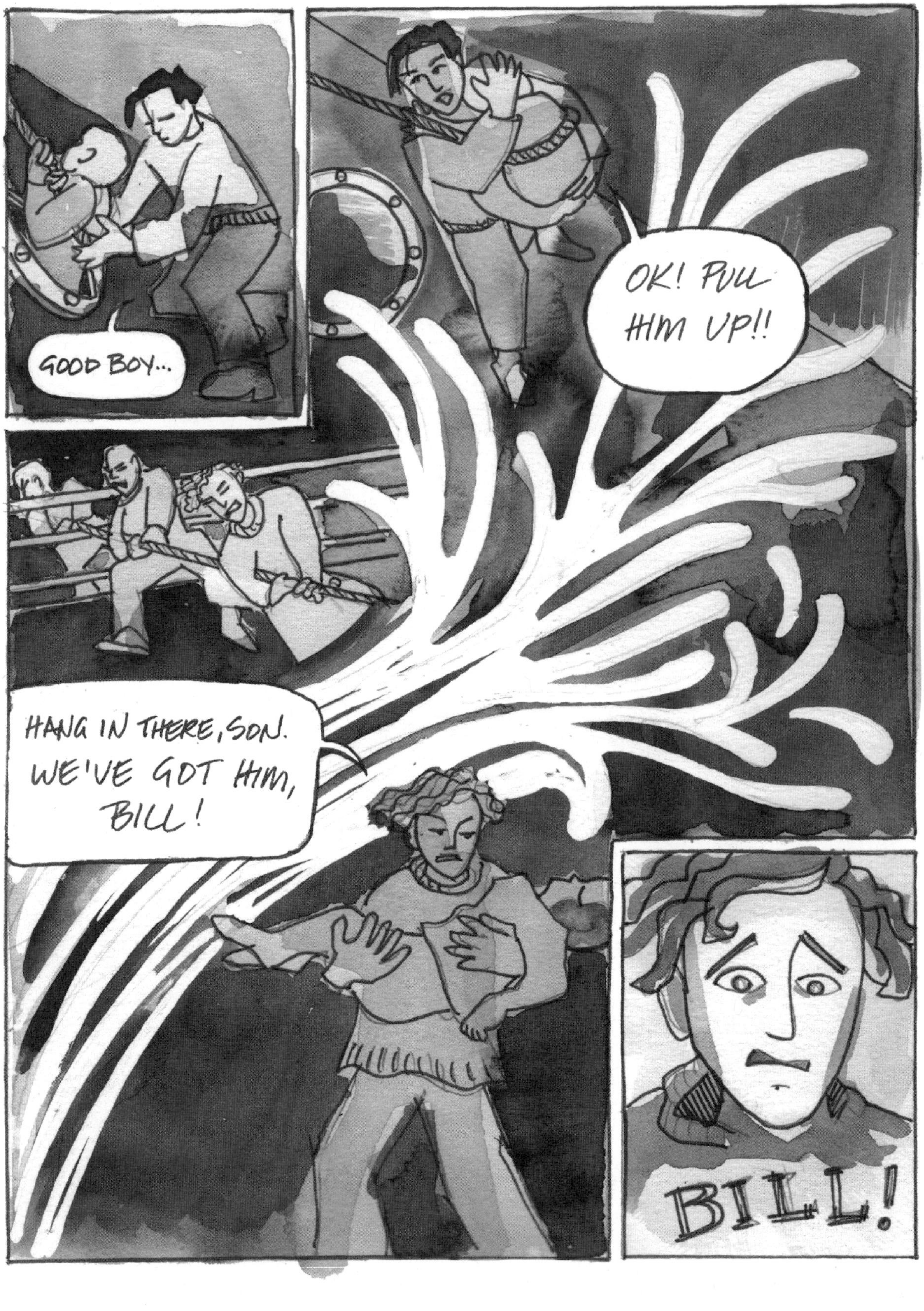
GOOD BOY...
OK! PULL HIM UP!!
HANG IN THERE, SON. WE'VE GOT HIM, BILL!
BILL!

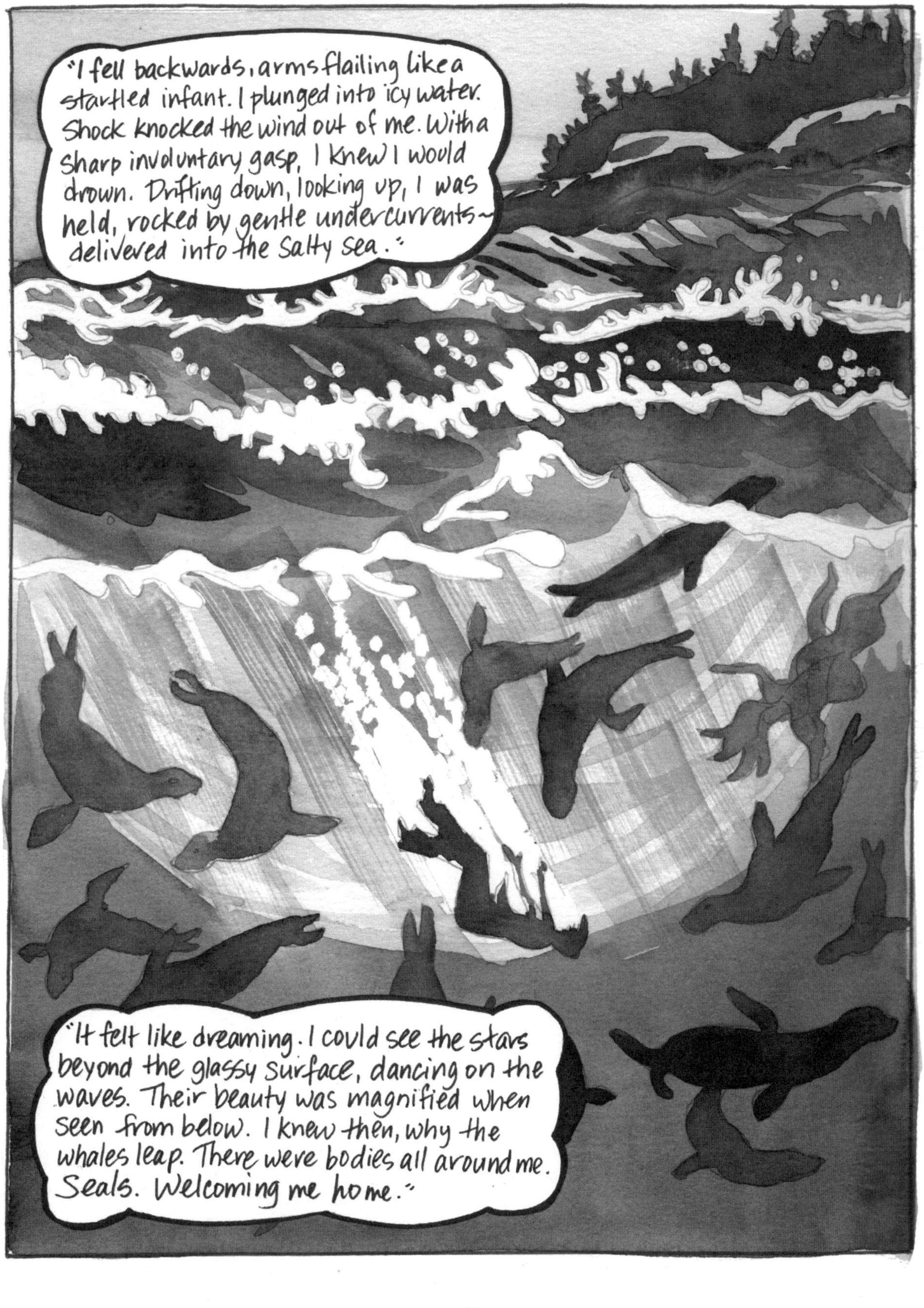
"I fell backwards, arms flailing like a startled infant. I plunged into icy water. Shock knocked the wind out of me. With a sharp involuntary gasp, I knew I would drown. Drifting down, looking up, I was held, rocked by gentle undercurrents~ delivered into the salty sea."
"It felt like dreaming. I could see the stars beyond the glassy surface, dancing on the waves. Their beauty was magnified when seen from below. I knew then, why the whales leap. There were bodies all around me. Seals. Welcoming me home."

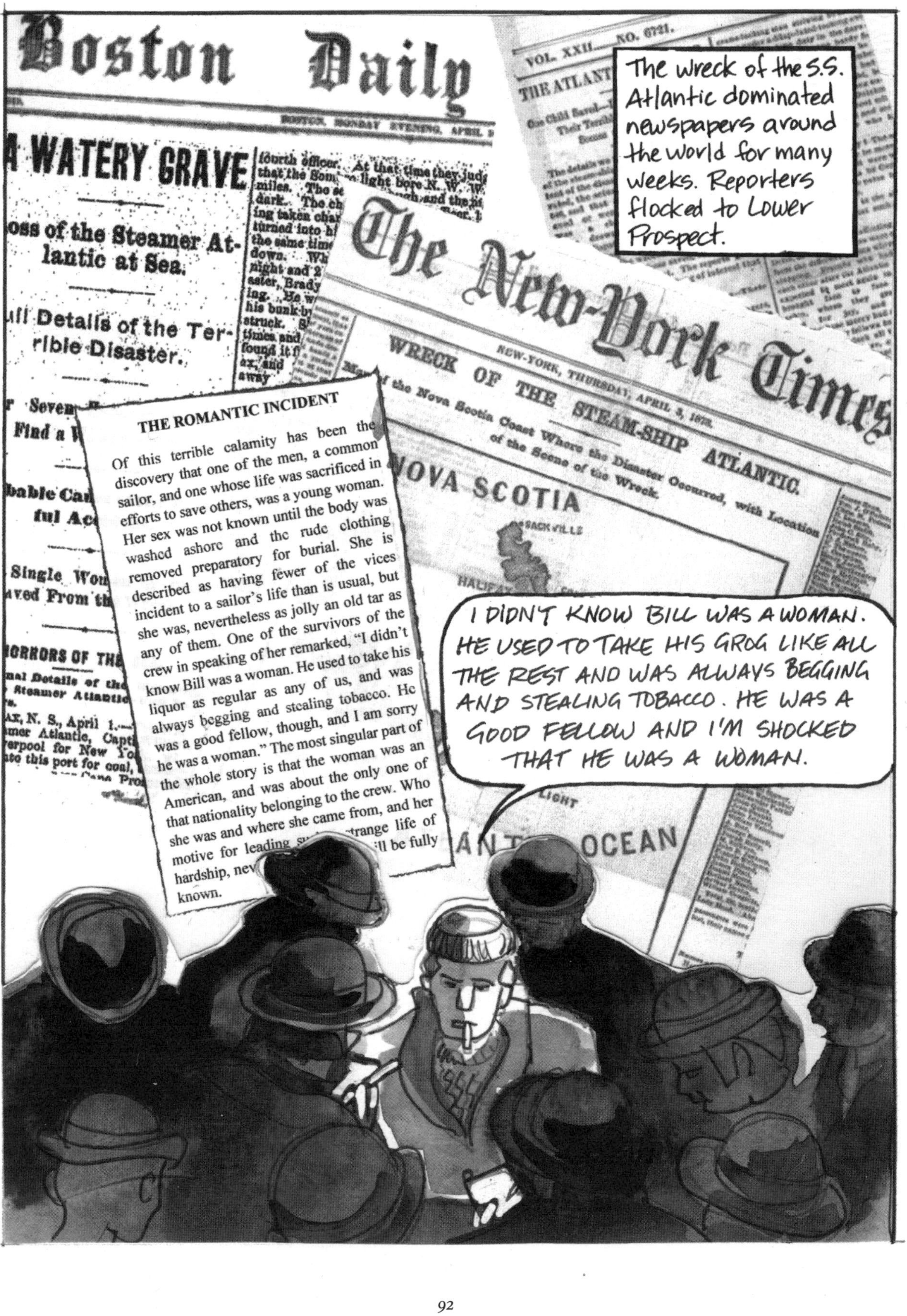
Boston Daily
A WATERY GRAVE
Loss of the Steamer Atlantic at Sea.
Full Details of the Terrible Disaster.
The wreck of the S.S. Atlantic dominated newspapers around the world for many weeks. Reporters flocked to Lower Prospect.
The New-York Times
NEW-YORK, THURSDAY, APRIL 3, 1873.
WRECK OF THE STEAM-SHIP ATLANTIC.
Map of the Nova Scotia Coast Where the Disaster Occurred, with Location of the Scene of the Wreck.
NOVA SCOTIA
THE ROMANTIC INCIDENT
Of this terrible calamity has been the
discovery that one of the men, a common
sailor, and one whose life was sacrificed in
efforts to save others, was a young woman.
Her sex was not known until the body was
washed ashore and the rude clothing
removed preparatory for burial. She is
described as having fewer of the vices
incident to a sailor's life than is usual, but
she was, nevertheless as jolly an old tar as
any of them. One of the survivors of the
crew in speaking of her remarked, "I didn't
know Bill was a woman. He used to take his
liquor as regular as any of us, and was
always begging and stealing tobacco. He
was a good fellow, though, and I am sorry
he was a woman." The most singular part of
the whole story is that the woman was an
American, and was about the only one of
that nationality belonging to the crew. Who
she was and where she came from, and her
motive for leading
hardship,
known.
I DIDN'T KNOW BILL WAS A WOMAN. HE USED TO TAKE HIS GROG LIKE ALL THE REST AND WAS ALWAYS BEGGING AND STEALING TOBACCO. HE WAS A GOOD FELLOW AND I'M SHOCKED THAT HE WAS A WOMAN.

The "Atlantic" Disaster.

WHERE SHALL THE DEAD BE BURIED!

AID FOR THE FISHERMEN

While the charitable public are thinking of how they can aid the survivors of the disaster, they should remember the people of Lower Prospect. We do not now refer to the acts of bravery which may merit rewards, but to the fact that the fishermen's families gave all the provisions they had to the shipwrecked people, and in many instances are now themselves in actual want. There could be no better way to manifest sympathy in the matter than to send down to Lower Prospect a quantity of provisions to refill the larders which were so cheerfully emptied to feed th̲ i̲stressed people. This is a̲ i̲ ̲ ̲ shoul̲ ̲ ̲

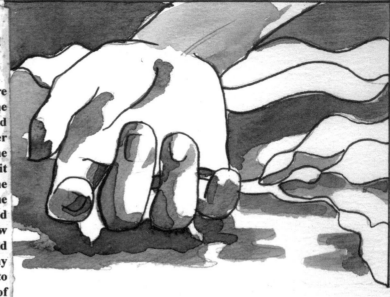

500 victims of one of the worst shipwrecks in history are interred in 2 mass graves in Lower Prospect and Terence Bay, Nova Scotia. The sailors placed a small wooden cross, inscribed Here lies Bill. She was a good sailor.

AUTHOR'S NOTES

This is the story of a person from an historical event in my community. This story intersects with my personal history as a feminist lesbian. I knew I wanted to tell this story as soon as I heard it when I served on the Board of Directors of the *SS Atlantic* Heritage Society and Park.

The 150th anniversary of the *SS Atlantic* wreck is 2023, during which there will be commemorative events. I believe it is imperative to preserve stories of the past, uncover and re-examine what has been forgotten, and reinstate what has been misrepresented.

In order to ensure that my work contributes to the uncovering of these stories without adding confusion or misrepresentation, I've decided to include the notes below.

THE WRECK AND THE RESCUES

SS Atlantic, a White Star Line passenger steamship, wrecked off the coast of Nova Scotia on April 1, 1873. Over time, that wreck has been largely overshadowed by the shipwreck of *Titanic*, the more famous White Star Line luxury steamship that sank off the coast of Newfoundland in 1912.

The heroic rescue and care of survivors by a tiny community is a proud example of human compassion for others, like the response to the downed Swiss Air Flight 111, and Gander Newfoundland's welcome of passengers during 9/11.

The crew of the ship and the villagers in the book are real people.

THE CREW

The names and actions of the crew are documented in the Official Inquiry.

The Canadian Official Inquiry into the wreck is a significant event in Canada's history as a nation. The inquiry findings were considered conclusive by the UK and USA, the countries of origin and destination.

THE VILLAGERS OF LOWER PROSPECT, UPPER PROSPECT, AND TERENCE BAY

The names and roles of the villagers have been researched and documented in Bob Chaulk's two excellent books: *SS Atlantic: The White Star Line's First Disaster at Sea* (co-authored with Greg Cochkanoff and published by Goose Lane Editions in 2009), and *Atlantic's Last Stop: Courage, Folly, and Lies in the White Star Line's Worst Disaster before Titanic* (published by Nimbus Publishing in 2021).

As a new Board member trying to acquaint myself with the story, I first encountered reference to 'The Female Sailor' in a Victorian novella called *Carrie Clancy; the Heroine of the Atlantic*. The novella asked the alluring question, "and who was the mysterious female sailor, who after saving several lives, was herself lost?". I asked Bob Chaulk if there was such a person, and he rolled his eyes, and rebuked the book as "pure drivel"! However, he did say that the newspapers of the time did indeed report on the discovery of the 'Female Sailor'!

Thus began four years of research and writing.

THE SAILOR

The protagonist of *Call Me Bill* is described in newspaper articles from *The Aberdeen Journal*, *Brisbane Times*, *Wilmington Morning Star*, *New-York Tribune*, *Halifax Morning Chronicle*, and more. Some excerpts are included in the book.

The newspaper article in which Maggie Armstrong states, "I call myself Billy when I put on my pantaloons" was written by Ralph Keeler, a correspondent for the *New-York Tribune*. In his autobiography, *Vagabond Adventures* (published in 1870 by Fields, Osgood & Co. of Boston), Keeler describes his own childhood as an orphan and runaway, finding work as a cabin boy on paddle wheelers on Lake Erie. Later he was a performer in minstrel shows on riverboats, singing, dancing, dressing as women, and in blackface (pretending to be a Black person on stage, now recognized as hurtful and offensive mockery of Black people). Ralph Keeler died mysteriously in 1873 enroute to Cuba, likely thrown overboard.

GENDER

Led by our current and ever-evolving understanding of gender, I do not presume to know the gender identity of our protagonist. Much of the story is told in the first person, based on Ralph Keeler's interview, in which our sailor identifies as Maggie. While it's best to ask people which pronouns they use, we can't do this in their case, because they've been dead for 150 years! So when the narrator speaks, they use "she/her" for sections when our protagonist self-identifies as Maggie, and "he/him" when they self-identify as Billy. It is a deliberate act of support to respond to people as they identify, without judgment or assumption. Although the historical reference materials refer to 'her' as the 'female sailor', I endeavor to blur that certainty by including current language.

HISTORIC CONTEXT: TRENTON, NEW JERSEY

The early story of Maggie Armstrong is set near Trenton, New Jersey, USA, during the 17 years before they embark on a life at sea. Trenton was a hub of activity for Quakers, who are known for their social activism and belief that all people are created equal.

It was also a hub of activity for the Civil War and the Women's Rights Movement. Women's rights activists (suffragists), Elizabeth Cady Stanton, and Susan B. Anthony were in Trenton in this era. Women paused their fight for equal rights during the Civil War (1861 -1865), when they shifted their focus to Abolition of Slavery. After the war, women resumed their fight for equal rights. Black men gained their right to vote in 1870, but women were still declared inferior. Sojourner Truth spoke out, 'I have worked as hard as any man! And ain't I a woman?!'

There are other historical accounts of women living as men. Some joined the army and fought in the Civil War. Others headed west, or like our sailor, headed out to sea. Some were trying to escape the restrictive roles available to women, and certainly some would be trans and gender-diverse if they lived today.

UNCERTAINTIES?

SS Atlantic wrecked on its 13th voyage. Maggie Armstrong arrived in New York two weeks before its 12th departure.

A sailor interviewed by a *New York Tribune* reporter said Bill was the only American among the crew.

I set out to tell the true story of the *SS Atlantic* wreck and the heroic rescue through the lens of the mysterious 'female sailor'. Newspapers provided facts, but did not, could not, recount the substance of the person. I recognized myself in this person, and I suspect many readers will too. This story presents the opportunity to explore identity, courage, and the radical imagination of a young person who took huge risks to occupy space that others would have had difficulty imagining.

Call Me Bill touches on issues that are still relevant today, including those being addressed by the Black Lives Matter, Me Too, Pride, and Occupy movements, as well as the Federal Pathway to address Missing and Murdered Indigenous Women, Girls and 2SLGBTQQIA+ People, and so many others. It has always been difficult for people who are sensitive to injustice to conform. I am one of those people. In *Call Me Bill*, I tried to illustrate the emotional experience of the sometimes painful process of self-discovery to self-acceptance.

WRITING AND ILLUSTRATING

I compiled the long version of this story while on retreat on the Bay of Fundy, and throughout the COVID-19 pandemic.

I wanted to activate readers' interest and imaginations around the important history of the *SS Atlantic*, and the heroic efforts of local Nova Scotian villagers. I believe pictures can accomplish this in a way that words cannot.

I chose to illustrate this story using grey watercolour washes, so the medium itself would be a metaphor for the vast range between binaries that we should all be encouraged to express. I allow the paint to flow across lines.

Many of my illustrations reference wood engravings and rare photographs of the event. I drew many others onsite as the rocky seascape of Lower Prospect Nova Scotia is largely unchanged today.

May the winds of change lift and shuffle the pages of history.

Lynette Richards has been cartooning her whole life. She chose stained glass as her professional medium because it was both a trade and an art. She was fully aware, too, that stained glass windows have used sequential narration for over 1000 years, and are essentially, early graphic novels! As a Craft Nova Scotia Master Artisan, Lynette is proud to have been selected to create large public art installations for the first Pride Library in Canada (UWO London ON), and the ArQuives (formerly the Canadian Lesbian and Gay Archives in Toronto).

Lynette Richards lives and works in Terence Bay Nova Scotia, where she owns and operates Rose Window Stained Glass and serves on the Board of Directors of the SS Atlantic Heritage Park and Society.